Country Towns of
VERMONT

Charming Small Towns and Villages to Explore

Stillman D. Rogers

Barbara Radcliffe Rogers

COUNTRY ROADS PRESS
NTC/Contemporary Publishing Group

Library of Congress Cataloging-in-Publication Data

Rogers, Stillman, 1939–
    Country towns of Vermont : charming small towns and villages to
explore / Stillman D. Rogers, Barbara Radcliffe Rogers.
        p.   cm. — (Country towns)
    ISBN 1-56626-195-3
    1. Vermont—Guidebooks.   2. Cities and towns—Vermont—Guidebooks.
I. Rogers, Barbara Radcliffe.   II. Title.   III. Series.
F47.3R645   1998
974.3—dc21   98-39742
                                        CIP

Cover and interior design by Nick Panos
Cover and interior illustrations and map copyright © Kathleen O'Malley

Published by Country Roads Press
A division of NTC/Contemporary Publishing Group, Inc.
4255 West Touhy Avenue, Lincolnwood (Chicago), Illinois 60646-1975 U.S.A.
Copyright © 1999 by Barbara and Stillman Rogers
Printed in the United States of America
International Standard Book Number: 1-56626-195-3
99 00 01 02 03 04 ML 18 17 16 15 14 13 12 11 10 9 8 7 6 5 4 3 2 1

*For Eric, with love and happy memories of
ski trails down Vermont mountainsides*

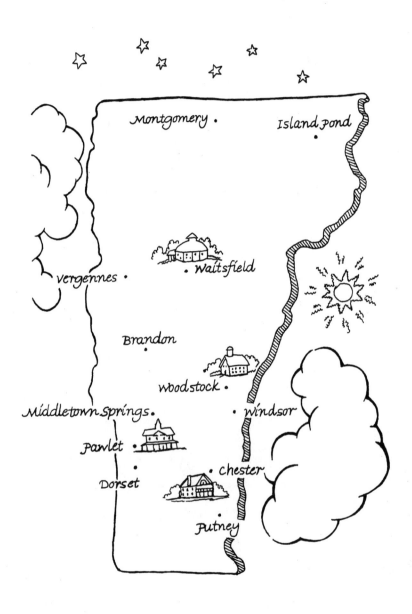

Montgomery •

Island Pond
•

• Waitsfield

vergennes •

Brandon

woodstock •

Middletown Springs •

• windsor

Pawlet •

• chester

Dorset •

Putney

CONTENTS

INTRODUCTION

As we write this introduction, Vermont is deep in snow, its country towns snug under feather beds, its waterfalls frozen to the rocks. Inside the towns are the same, whether the seasons paint them white, green, or orange on the outside. And even in the time of year we call, with characteristic directness, mud season, the towns are attractive to look at and to be in.

As they lie deep in winter snow, many of them swarm with skiers, and many others close to popular ski areas welcome tired skiers to the firesides of their inns and restaurants. For the "white gold" sustains the Vermont economy in winter just as its legendary maple leaves do in the fall and its moderate temperatures and fresh mountain air do in the summer. People like to come to Vermont, in any season.

But no matter how deeply the life of a town seems rooted in welcoming tourists, there is still a life underneath, a life that goes on year-round, in snowless winters when the skiers don't come, in hard times and good. It is the real fiber of a town, the school board, selectmen (no, in Vermont all towns have not neutered their vocabulary, either officially or colloquially), the fire department, the library, the churches, the historical society, the general store, the farms, the manufacturing plants, the neighbors, and the families all woven together into a fabric far stronger and far richer than the idyllic community a passing traveler sees.

It is this Vermont we have tried to capture in *Country Towns of Vermont*. Through the stories, the history, the buildings, the local places and activities of 12 of these towns, we have tried to show what makes Vermont what it is. Perhaps it is true that you must live here to understand Vermont, but we think you can go a long way by understanding how Vermont began, who the first settlers were, and how they carved their farms tree by tree out of a wilderness. We think the stories of how the Green Mountain Boys got started (it wasn't to fight the British, by the way) and why Vermont is not a part of either New York or New Hampshire tell a lot about the character of the state.

Or does it simply contribute to the myth? Is Vermont any different from its neighbors? Is it just possibly America's first and longest-running PR campaign? We don't think so. No matter how many silly movies and sitcoms either parody the state or reduce it to clichés, there had to be good material to work with. There has to be character in a place before it can produce characters. There's a lot more to Vermont than "yup" and "nope."

Why and how have we chosen these particular towns to tell the story of Vermont? Clearly not from a map, since we have not scattered them evenly throughout the state. There are more, for example, in the Valley of Vermont than in the Northeast Kingdom. Does this mean we like the valley better, or that its towns are more interesting? Far from it. Given our druthers, we'd spend our year lost in the spruce forests with the moose, and paddling through the remote reaches of the Missisquoi delta in a canoe.

Instead, we chose on the grounds of which towns had a story to tell that showed some side of life, some piece of history, some economic reality, some quirk of personality that, while being interesting, was also representative of the state as a whole.

When we started to choose, we thought we already knew the state pretty well. We'd hiked, skied, camped, driven, and canoed in every corner, been in nearly every town and city. We'd slept in the B&Bs and knew a lot of the chef-restaurateurs by name. We knew Hyde Park from Green River, and a town lattice from a Burr bridge. If we weren't seventh generation, we weren't flatlanders, either. (Both cliché terms, by the way, which we hear more from outsiders than we do from insiders.)

But one looks at a place differently when writing about it, so we set out to travel the state with an eye to selecting our towns. The problem with that was finding a town that *didn't* belong in the book. Each crossroads, each village green, each hardscrabble farm settlement offered a story uniquely its own, and each provided a view of the whole Vermont.

We began, together and individually, to defend the place of certain towns on our growing list. We debated, each defending our favorites. The list got longer, not shorter, until it seemed we would never narrow it to a dozen. But as we traveled, as we ate lunch in the diners, bought groceries at crossroad stores, sat over coffee with innkeepers, lingered in tiny local historical society museums, listened to people who had lived close to a century in their town, hiked to the cellar holes of long-forgotten villages, and discussed the project with friends all over the state, some towns finally began to emerge as clearer choices.

As the time approached when we had to begin writing, we made our decisions, slowly and painfully, but finally. We have left out towns we ached to include, chosen towns others will certainly disagree with. We can't even begin to list those that almost made it and missed, not because they were less interesting, but because another town brought a greater variety of themes to the book as a whole. Sometimes it was a line so fine that a single building made the difference. Waitsfield tipped the balance over neighboring Warren because of one barn, a rare remaining round one. And since, like Napoleon's army, we march on our stomachs, Pawlet edged out Fair Haven's slate quarries by feeding us moose meatballs and venison sausage (over a span of many years, mind you).

And what of those others that didn't make it? There's only one solution. Watch your neighborhood bookstore for *Coun-*

try Towns of Vermont II or *Son of Vermont Country Towns* or *Country Towns of Vermont Strikes Again.*

Meanwhile, enjoy these towns, read about them, visit them, use them as a base for exploring others just as interesting. And if you notice that the one major facet of Vermont that we have not emphasized is its vast and numerous natural attractions—its rich birdlife, unique bogs, dramatic gorges and waterfalls—it is not because we found them less interesting or exciting a part of Vermont. It is because we sought to avoid overlapping with our other book on the state, *Natural Wonders of Vermont,* also published by Country Roads. If Vermont's unbelievably rich natural world excites you as it does us, you will want to travel with both books at your side. Together, we think, they will lead you to know Vermont.

1

DORSET:
SPLIT BY A MARBLE
MOUNTAIN

When New Hampshire's Royal Governor Benning Wentworth, with a flourish of his quill, created Dorset out of the 36 square miles of land north of Manchester (which His Excellency had created with the same pen only moments before), little did he know, or probably care, what problems he would create in succeeding centuries for the town with a mountain down its middle. The two fine valleys he united in this political marriage were separated by the bundling board of Mt. Aeolus, Mt. Neetop, and Dorset Mountain, each over three thousand feet high and connected in a ridge with saddles only slightly lower than their summits.

Each of the parallel valleys had its attractions, and in them grew separate villages. They are still separate today, although a year-round road, paved most of the way, runs over the shoulder, south of both villages, forming a nine-mile U-curve between them. Those mountains, whatever problems they were to bring, were also to be the source of Dorset's fame and fortune.

To further complicate communications, the center of the wider, west valley (where Route 30 runs today) was cut by a giant swamp. Mother Myrick, the valley's midwife, lived on West Road, and when she was needed to deliver a baby on the east side, the family signaled her by banging on a log. She and her mule would then cross the swamp. Mother Myrick Mountain, on the west side of town, is named for her.

Wentworth was not so concerned with the problems of the villages that would grow there as he was with nailing down his claim to land over which jurisdiction had not been clearly defined. While Governor Clinton of New York viewed his own patent from King Charles as clear proof of his control of all lands west of the Connecticut River, Wentworth claimed that the line was a northward continuation of the boundary between Massachusetts and New York. He ordered the land west of the Connecticut River surveyed and marked into segments six miles square, and he began making grants. Within two years he granted over one hundred of these towns to settlers who had begun carving farmsteads out of the forests. Governor Clinton pleaded his case to the king.

No stranger to British politics, Wentworth named his townships for influential people at court; Dorset he named for the Duke of Dorset, in the expectation that the duke would whisper kind words into the ear of the king in support of Wentworth's claims. Meanwhile, New Yorkers, accompanied by sheriffs, also began to claim title to lands settled in Dorset and surrounding grants, lands painstakingly cleared and planted by the settlers who lived on them.

Enter the Green Mountain Boys. This band of rowdies, led by Ethan Allen, came to the defense of the settlers and harassed the New Yorkers wherever they appeared. Expert riflemen and woodsmen, and unabashedly defiant of any New York authority, they kept the situation at a standoff, also sending packing all the new grantees New York was sending into the unchartered northern towns. There is little question that the Green Mountain Boys and their friends had an eye to the future, realizing that their relative distance between the capitals at Portsmouth and Albany would make it easier for them to part with New Hampshire later than with New York. They had an eye to a separate province.

With the outbreak of the Revolution in April of 1775, and the capture of Fort Ticonderoga by the Green Mountain Boys, New York and the settlers of the New Hampshire Grants formed an uneasy truce and joined forces against the British. The Continental Congress sanctioned the recognition of the Green Mountain Boys as an independent military force, and they met on July 26, 1775, in Cephas Kent's Tavern on West Road in Dorset. They elected their officers, choosing Seth Warner as their commander.

At a subsequent meeting in the tavern, they further asserted that while they wholeheartedly supported the cause of freedom, they intended to do it on their own terms, and not as a part of New York. Those who defend Dorset as "the birthplace of Vermont" point to this statement and to the subsequent resolution inviting all landholders in the New Hampshire Grants to join in a separate "Association." Which, of course, they did, but at meetings adjourned to Westminster and Windsor, where the actual vote was taken and the name Vermont chosen.

If you drive along West Road today, you will see a marble marker at the corner of Nichols Road, just north of the Marble West Inn, commemorating the meetings of the Committee of Safety. The Cephas Kent Tavern stood at this corner.

The rugged farmers of Dorset and their neighbors soon had a worse threat than New York sheriffs to consider. General Burgoyne sent a force, bolstered by Indians friendly to the British, in an attempt to clear the valley. Word of the troops' approach was brought by northern settlers fleeing their burning farms.

In Dorset, Mrs. Titus Sykes was doing her laundry when the alarm came, and she grabbed her child and fled on horseback, making her way back to her parents' home in Connecticut. She didn't even empty out the washtub, which was lucky, since her wedding ring had slipped off into it. She found it there when she returned four months later—or so they say. We'll meet the Sykes family again, as Dorset storekeepers and benefactors who, generations later, sent a son off to the Civil War. There are still Sykeses listed in the Dorset phone book, although the general store is now operated by someone else.

Life was brutally hard for the settlers. The frontier women weren't the dainty ladies who paraded their imported finery on the streets of Boston and New Haven. They wore rough homespun, worked beside the men, and together they carved out the fields that would later become the manicured lawns of Dorset. Life didn't change much after the war ended and after Vermont became the 14th state in 1791, but at least they were safe from marauding redcoats and New York sheriffs, and the land they tilled was their own. Money was a rare sight, and beef, pork, sheep, rye, wheat, and corn were considered legal tender. Landowners could pay their taxes with grain, and their wives could trade spun wool or handknit socks for sugar at the general store.

If all this seems like a very large introduction to the small town of Dorset, it is because it is also an introduction to the history of the state of Vermont. Dorset, although very different in many ways, shares the history and the ups and downs of many of its fellow towns. Disputes over land grants, problems caused by the flat-map style of the early surveys, the privations of its early settlers, even fluctuations of its economy and population in concert with the rising and falling fortunes of the quarries and farming—all of these themes will echo in the stories of other towns. Dorset not only offers a microcosm of this story, but it was the scene of the early meetings that shaped Vermont and laid the foundation for its becoming a state.

Although Dorset's early history parallels that of many other towns in this state, its recent history is uniquely its own, shaped by its location, geography, and the character of the people who went there, both as settlers and in the centuries that followed.

But we get ahead of our story. The first major economic wave to reach Dorset was sheep. The town is thought to be the place where sheep were first introduced to the region, and they evidently found a hospitable home there, since their numbers quickly grew.

Meanwhile, in 1785, the first commercial marble quarry in North America opened in Dorset. (It was also the year that Dorset's first public school opened.) For the next century, marble was increasingly to rule the economy, society, and even the appearance of Dorset. The mountain that divided the town contained a rich band of high-quality building stone. The first products were hearthstones and headstones. At first these were sold to itinerant stonecutters who traveled with wagonloads of them, stopping at farmhouses, where family burial plots were common. They would sell the stones and stay to carve the inscriptions.

Later, stone was carried by oxcart and horse-drawn wagons to the Champlain and Hudson Canal landing, from which it could be shipped by boat. With the opening of the small Manchester, Dorset, and Granville Railroad (whose initials caused it to be known locally as the Mud, Dirt, and Gravel Railroad), stone was carried south to Manchester Depot, where it was cut into blocks and column segments before shipping to building sites.

It was here that the columns were cut for the New York Public Library, whose facing stone also came from the Norcross-West quarry. If you look around the parking area of J. K. Adams woodworking factory, just south of Dorset village on Route 30, you will see the remains of the blocks from which these library columns were cut. (J. K. Adams is worth a stop to shop for cutting boards, salad bowls, countertops, and other fine wooden accessories. Check the seconds for even better bargains.)

In 1851, the main railway line opened to Dorset, passing through the eastern of the two valleys and the village of East Dorset, where by this time several more quarries had opened. East Dorset thrived and grew as the terminus. Irish workers, who had left their homes following the Great Potato Famine in the 1840s, helped build the railroad (by 1850 there were fifteen thousand Irish living in Vermont), and many stayed to work in the quarries. In 1874, St. Jerome's Church was dedicated, the first Roman Catholic parish in the area. It still serves the towns of Dorset and Rupert. Unlike other quarry towns, which became virtual little melting pots, Dorset's immigrant population was almost entirely Irish.

East Dorset, from its beginning, had a different flavor from the western village. It was a gritty, blue-collar town. The quarry owners lived on the west side of the mountain, the workers on the east. While farmhouses in Dorset took in summer guests weary of the city, the Mt. Aeolus Inn, across from the railway station in East Dorset, put up salesmen and travelers breaking their train journey for the night. During Prohibition, the inn thrived as a stopping-off place for those who could afford to travel to Montreal to drink, and in those tonier days

catered to the likes of Charles Lindbergh and Myrna Loy. The East Dorset stop was just halfway between New York and Montreal.

Earlier, around the turn of the century, before it assumed the title of Mt. Aeolus Inn, it was the Wilson House, catering to lumbermen and quarry workers, and operated by "the Widow Wilson." Her grandson, Bill, was born in 1895 in a little room in the back of the first floor, where a bar was later set up. He served in France during World War I, and returned to a position on Wall Street. His addiction to alcohol grew worse until, in 1935, he and Dr. Robert Smith (Dr. Bob), a native of St. Johnsbury, Vermont, developed the 12-Step recovery process and founded Alcoholics Anonymous.

Their story is well known to the hundreds of recovered and recovering who visit the Wilson House each year. Once again an inn, but one with a mission, the Wilson House was rescued from near collapse in 1987 by Ozzie and Sandy Lepper, who have formed a foundation to restore and preserve it, not as a museum, but as a living memorial. It is not advertised as an inn, although its bright, cheery guest rooms are often filled, and the Wilson House is supported entirely through income from rooms and by private donations. The house is staffed and maintained by volunteers; AA and Al-Anon groups meet there regularly. Across the green, in front of the church, is the house where Bill W. spent part of his childhood with his maternal grandparents; the house is open to visitors.

Bill W. and his wife, Lois, are buried in the East Dorset Cemetery, south of the village on Route 7A, about 1.7 miles from the Wilson House. Bill's simple headstone is the eighth on the left from the tree stump toward the rear of the cemetery. The path is a well-worn one.

Just north of the junction of Route 7A and U.S. 7 is a relic of the Dorset iron industry, which thrived in the 1820s. A short distance down Benedict Road, which branches left from Morse Hill Road (the one that goes over the mountain to connect the two villages), almost directly behind the Christmas Tree Bed and Breakfast, is a stone and brick iron furnace, the best preserved in Vermont. The foundry there operated for about 10 years, producing stoves and plows. The Conroys, who built the cozy ski-lodge style B&B, don't mind visitors coming into their driveway for a better view of the furnace, but they caution that loose stones inside the furnace make it dangerous to enter.

Marble quarrying reached its peak in the 1880s, employing two hundred Dorset residents—10 percent of the population—and an equal number from surrounding towns. It equaled farming as a source of employment. Between 1785 and 1920, over 15.5 million cubic feet of marble was taken from the 25 or so quarries that cut into the hillsides of Dorset, most of them in the slopes of the mountain that separated the two villages.

The earliest of these quarries is easy to see—in fact, you can swim in it. Just north of the intersection of West Road and Route 30, on the east side of the road, you will see a wide place to park; in the summer it will probably be filled with cars. In clear view of the road is the quarry, now filled with springwater.

While the quarry was still active, the workers shut down the equipment one evening, leaving it and the mule teams in the bottom of the pit as usual. When they arrived the next morning, they found the pit half full of water, which was rising rapidly. They had hit a spring without realizing it. By then it was too late to rescue anything or stop the flow, so they just let it fill. It is estimated to be about 110 feet deep. To the right of the quarry is a stone building dating from 1773, now part of a private home. It was built to house the workers, and is thought to be the oldest marble house in the United States.

Dorset's quarries provided marble for the Jefferson Memorial and for the columns of the D.A.R. Building in Washington, D.C., as well as for the Harvard Medical School and countless other public and private buildings. Closer to home, it provided stone for Dorset structures. One Federal-style home, known as "The Old Stone House," was built entirely of rough-cut marble, and enlarged early in this century. It stands alongside Dorset West Road, which was the original main road, not far from the site of Cephas Kent's Tavern. The marble-stepped garden can be seen behind the house, rising up a hill to a pergola.

Most Dorset homes, however, even the grander ones, were built of wood, on foundations of marble block, and decorated with marble embellishments. One of the finest examples of this construction is also on West Road, a bit north of the stone house. Now Marble West Inn, it was built by George Holley, himself an important man in the marble industry, for his daughter at her marriage to Spafford West, founder of the Norcross-West Marble Company. Built in 1840, in Greek Revival style, the house has foundations, porches, steps, walkways, fireplaces, and front columns of marble.

The house is representative of Dorset in another way, too. The elaborate stenciling in the entrance hall was done by the premier modern stencil artist, Adele Bishop, a former Dorset resident and friend of a West descendant. (The house stayed in the West family nearly 150 years, until it was converted into an inn in 1985.) Adele Bishop was one of several well-known artists and writers who made their summer (or year-round) homes in Dorset. This artistic tradition is still strong today, with several well-known artists living there—including the muralist Dean Fausett and the art historian Hendrik van Loon.

It was largely due to the summer people and the art community that Dorset escaped the fate of many small towns when the building stone industry died. It was their interest—and their money—that renovated and preserved the old farms and town houses. The tradition of summering in Dorset had begun in the mid-19th century, when local farmers took in summer guests to help make the ends of their budget meet. As more people came looking for rooms, the farmhouses were improved and kept up to attract the visitors.

The Inn at West View Farm began this way, offering a few rooms to summer guests, and although it has grown into a full-service inn with two dining rooms, it still offers rooms in the beautifully restored original farmhouse—having added modern plumbing and a few other improvements. The hearty farm dinners have been replaced with one of Vermont's finest menus—a selection that includes dishes such as rosemary quail and pan-seared sesame shrimp.

The first known summer visitors were the Reverend George and Elizabeth Payson Prentiss in 1866. He was pastor of the Church of the Covenant in New York, and she was a well-known writer. By the turn of the century, Dorset published a little brochure to advertise the beauties of the town as a summer getaway.

These summer people took an active interest in the town. One lady from Philadelphia visited the schools regularly, donating equipment, giving prizes to students and inviting them to her home for readings. Summer residents researched the town's history, and donated antiquities to the historical society. They bought homes and fixed them up, then retired in Dorset.

They not only preserved Dorset's history; they took in strays from other towns' histories. Charles Wade, a livery operator, heard of the hundreds of homes that were slated to be flooded in the construction and filling of the Quabbin Reservoir in central Massachusetts. In the depth of the Great Depression, he bought 30 of these for next to nothing and hired a crew of 30 or so craftsmen and carpenters to move and reassemble them. At least eight were sold to summer people in Dorset. Coincidentally, several of the buildings came from the town of Enfield, Massachusetts, where a number of Dorset's original settlers also came from.

One of the buildings, the former Enfield Congregational Church chapel, on the main street, is pointed out in the excellent recorded walking tour of Dorset provided to visitors by the historical society. Not only is the tour interesting, but the society is open on Saturday mornings year-round. (You will appreciate just how rare this is in small towns, whose museums are usually open only in the summer.) Pick up a tape recorder and book of photographs—thoughtfully provided to help you spot each building and landmark—at the society's museum diagonally opposite the Dorset Inn.

While there, look through the collections, which include rare examples of Fenton pottery, which later gained fame as Bennington pottery. Along with posters for long-ago pie suppers, farm implements, and a fascinating collection of old photographs of the quarries, is the wooden splint worn home from Gettysburg by a descendant of the same Mrs. Sykes who almost lost her wedding ring. In 1994, the Sykes family had a reunion in Dorset, including some Midwest relatives who had never seen the town. They spent hours in the society's genealogical collections and bought Vermont cheese from Peltier's Store, which had been owned by several generations of their ancestors.

A walk through the aisles of Peltier's General Store tells a lot about Dorset residents and visitors. Peltier's has it all, and for everybody—from tennis balls and basmati rice to Bisquick and mason jar lids.

A glance at Dorset's rather ambitious town newspaper, *The Dorset Country Journal*, tells even more. It tells of plans for the Garden Weekend in June, when private homes in both villages open their gardens to the public for the benefit of the town's community services. It tells of public-spirited people who have served the town well, of summer resident Dom DeLuise, of the town's Father's Day program and the schedule for the Dorset Theater Festival, of the recycling program, and of the new "Welcome Home" program that offers a package of gifts to newcomers in town. There's even the recipe for the sweet onions served by Cat's Dogs, the homegrown lunch cart with the green awning. Like Dorset itself, *The Dorset Country Journal* is rich in variety and interest, far beyond its size.

Places to See, Eat, and Stay

The Marble West Inn, Dorset West Rd., Dorset 05251; (802) 867-4155 or (800) 453-7629. The inn serves full dinners on weekends to overnight guests who reserve in advance.

Inn at West View Farm, Route 30, Dorset 05251; (802) 867-5715. You should make reservations for dinner here, even in slow seasons, since its consistent quality keeps the dining room busy.

Barrows House, Main St., Dorset 05251; (802) 867-4455 or (800) 639-1620. An inn and dining room.

Christmas Tree Bed and Breakfast, Benedict Rd., RR 1, Box 582, East Dorset 05253; (802) 362-4889.

The Wilson House, Village St., East Dorset 05253; (802) 362-5524.

The Dorset Historical Society, P.O. Box 52, Dorset 05251; (802) 867-4450. Open year-round Saturday, 10 A.M. to noon, or by appointment. While there, look for the thorough and well-written town history.

2

PAWLET: MAKING A LIVING FROM THE LAND

(PAWLET IS 26 MILES SOUTH OF RUTLAND ON ROUTE 133.)

The riches of its land brought the first settlers to Pawlet, and they have sustained the town into the present century. Its fertile valley farmland attracted families from Massachusetts and Connecticut to the rolling countryside along the Mettawee River, where they cleared the land we still see farmed today.

The terms of the grants made by Royal Governor Benning Wentworth were that the grantee must clear, plant, and cultivate five acres for each 50 acres in the grant within five years. Of the trees, all mast pines (those straight and tall enough, with a diameter of 24 inches or more) must be reserved for the Royal Navy. After 10 years, a yearly rent of one shilling was due for each hundred acres.

Although some settlers moved the whole family directly to the wilderness, it was more likely that a man would arrive the first spring to clear enough land for a house and garden and perhaps begin building the house from logs he had cut. He then returned to spend the winter in the town where he had left his family. In the spring they would all travel north to the new land, bringing household goods and whatever livestock they owned.

From that point, the couple—and any children old enough—worked together to get in a garden, plant hay and corn for feed, clear more land, build the house, tend and harvest the crops, and store them for the winter. It was a lot for a small group to accomplish in a short summer and without support of neighbors or an extended family. But these little farms that slowly appeared in Pawlet's valley forests grew year by year and thrived in the fertile bottomland soil.

In 1768, only six years after the first settler arrived, a gristmill was built at the falls of the Flower River, close to its junction with the Mettawee, the beginnings of the village we see today. Soon after, the first tavern opened. By 1770, a dozen farms were scattered throughout the valley.

In 1777, a company of militia men was organized here, under the command of Samuel Herrick. Known as Herrick's Rangers, they were nicknamed "The Terror of the Tories." Pawlet became a center of activity for the Vermont regiments in the fall of that year, as twenty-five hundred troops under the command of General Benjamin Lincoln camped there in preparation for the storming of Mount Defiance, near Fort Ticonderoga. He sent five hundred men to Ticonderoga and five hundred to Mount Independence, across the lake. These forces captured war stores that included horses, two hundred longboats, several gunboats, an armed sloop, wagons, and prisoners, at the same time freeing over one hundred Continental troops who had been captured earlier. Captain Ebenezer Allen's company of Vermont Rangers scaled and captured Mount Defiance from the British.

These losses, plus the strong presence of so many troops assembled in Pawlet, helped to prevent the British from sending supplies and reinforcements to General Burgoyne at Saratoga. It also prevented him from retreating to Canada, all of which contributed to his surrender at Saratoga less than a month later. On the east side of Route 30 in North Pawlet, in front of a one-story brick schoolhouse, is a stone monument with a plaque recounting the story of that fall's military activities.

After the Revolution, many of those who had been headquartered in Pawlet decided to settle there. Historians don't draw any relationship between this influx of Green Mountain Boys and the fact that by 1782, the number of taverns had grown to six, nearly one-fourth the number in the entire county and more than in Tinmouth, which was the shire town.

The new settlers had a slightly easier time hewing their homesteads out of the forest than did their predecessors. Often they could stay with friends or families already settled there, and the small community could provide help when it was needed. Others came to work on the growing farms in order to buy land—one or two years' work on a farm could earn a man enough to buy one hundred acres.

There was very little specialization in these early farms. Each family grew what it needed, including flax for clothing. The forests provided maple sugar and fuel, and the abundant wood ash left from fires was made into potash, which could be sold to buy finished goods. In addition to potash, many farmers sold wheat, which was the first true cash crop in the valley. Some sold farm animals to the drovers who came through regularly to provide meat for Boston and other cities.

By the turn of the century, these farms had changed little, except that there were more frame houses and fewer log cabins. Several of the homes built in the 1790s to replace original log cabins are standing today. One of these, built by a veteran of the Revolution in 1795, is an elegant Federal home, the central of the three large houses that sit below the road level on Route 30, just south of the village center.

Pawlet is exceedingly rich in well-kept examples of homes from this era, several of which are on remote roads. One is a short way out Danby Road on the left, off Route 133; another, an especially handsome brick, is on Herrick Brook Road, also off Route 133. A third, which shares the unusual broad facade of the previous two and is thought to be the work of the same local architect, is the first house on the west side of Route 30 as you cross the line into Pawlet, traveling north from Rupert. It is now identified by a sign as the Woodlawn Farm and, even passing by it on the road, you can see its splendid doorway.

Replacing their early sheds, most farmers built barns used for housing livestock and storing hay and equipment, as well as for chores such as threshing grain. They could build their own with the help of neighbors or have one built for less than 50 dollars.

After 1825, the bottom fell out of the market for wheat, as the opening of the Champlain and Erie Canals brought in western wheat at prices the small-yield Vermont farms couldn't compete with. Some farmers left to join those in the new lands of the West; others stayed and turned their rolling wheat fields into pastures for sheep. New tariffs had made American-grown wool competitive. Several farms in Pawlet had already been raising sheep, having imported the Merino breed, highly prized for its superior long-staple wool. By 1840, Pawlet had more than twenty thousand head of sheep.

All that wool had to be processed, and Flower Brook and the Mettawee provided waterpower. Soon small mills in Pawlet were able to full, card, spin, and weave the wool fiber into fabric. The village became a small industrial center, which in turn attracted more mills, including a tannery and a mill for making linseed into oil for varnish. Corn, rye, and apples were processed into spirited drinks in no less than five distilleries (perhaps to supply all those taverns). By 1830, Pawlet rivaled Rutland as a center for manufacturing and commerce.

It was in these years that the buildings we now see clustered tightly around the dam in the village center were built. The Fitch Tavern perched on the brink of the gorge at the crossroads. The building now houses one of our all-time favorite general stores, Mach's. Opposite it, now almost flush with the edge of Route 30, was a store and post office with a classic porch. Next to that was a house with a porch and balcony, also still standing. The Congregational Church was built in 1841. The brick Federal house facing Mach's General Store was built in 1800. A later building, but blending well with the row of porched buildings, is the Masonic Temple, whose slate roof is patterned in Masonic emblems.

When the development of the refrigerated railway car made shipping fluid milk possible, dairy farming increased, gradually replacing sheep in importance. In 1864, Consider Bardwell built the first cheese factory in the state on his farm in West Pawlet, and a year later it became a cooperative; factory-made cheese slowly edged out farm cheese. Dairy farmers supplied the milk and shared in the factory's profits. Bardwell was already known for the axes and other tools he made as a sideline to farming.

The Bardwell farm, complete with many of its original buildings, is intact today. It stretches along Route 153, south of the village of West Pawlet, one of the finest examples of 19th-century farm complexes in the state. The manmade pond in its center furnished power for the ax workshop, and around it stand the farmhouse, built in 1814, a smokehouse, a schoolhouse, a granary, and pig houses, all built of brick and constructed before 1860. These and other buildings are in excellent condition and give a good view of what these farms looked like a century and a half ago.

The opening of the cooperative meant that much of the work of cheese making shifted away from the farm, making it possible—and profitable—for dairies to increase their herds. Huge new barns replaced smaller ones, with multi-story cribs for silage inside them. Two fine examples of these remain in Pawlet. One, on Route 133 northeast of the village, not far from the town line, has a cupola and is easily identi-fied as White Column Farm, now raising registered highland cattle, whose shaggy brown shapes can usually be seen in the adjoining pasture. The other is on Route 149, toward the New York border, about halfway between its junction with Route 30 and the quarry.

Travelers approaching Pawlet from the north on Route 30 drive past several impressive farms, their clusters of buildings with barns and giant silos standing close to the road. The rolling fields of rich alluvial soil, which once grew wheat, then pastured sheep, are still an active part of Vermont's agricultural heritage.

When the railroad opened a line paralleling the New York border along the western edge of town, a small depot was built at the crossroads, almost on the border. The village of West Pawlet began to grow around this depot (the present depot was constructed later), but was never more than a quiet little settlement until 1870. In that year Rising and Nelson began quarrying green slate from the vein that extends from Sudbury to Rupert.

Nearly every house in West Pawlet was built between the opening of the quarries and about 1910, most in the last decade of the century. In 1890 an entire street was laid out, appropriately called New Street, where the stoneworkers built their homes. Here and elsewhere in West Pawlet, you will see wooden gabled homes in the style known as Queen

Anne, with fancy porches and a variety of decorative trims. Nearly every house in town has a slate roof, many of them multicolored.

Few villages are so clearly representative of a single era as West Pawlet; one has the feeling that the town was dropped there, complete, from a century ago. In the middle of this tightly compacted village are two classic brick commercial buildings from the turn of the century. The cornices of the one on the right are of pressed metal. Remnants of the advertising message that was painted on its side in three-foot letters are still legible: "PAINE's CELERY COMPOUND MAKES PEOPLE WELL." Before the small store to the right was built, the sign was in full view of passengers on the Rutland and Washington Railroad as the train pulled out of the depot.

The tracks are gone and the right-of-way is now a public trail for hiking, bicycling, and cross-country skiing. In the winter, snowmobiles can use it, but no motorized vehicles are allowed the rest of the year.

At the northern edge of the village, extending literally into the backyards of the houses, is one of the tailings piles, a mountain of slate scrap. Just past it, on either side of the road, are the deep quarry holes, surrounded by their slate walls. The giant hills of tailings continue along the road, held back in place by retaining walls built of stacked slate. When passing through the village from the south, this stone wasteland comes as a bit of a shock, but it is immediately followed by an attractive neighborhood called, for some reason we're not able to fathom, Spruce Gum. Don't plan to have lunch in West Pawlet; there is no commercial activity except for Dutchy's Store, a couple of offices, and an art and antique shop just past the depot on Route 29, where they sell bureaus and other furniture painted with clever and amusing barnyard scenes. Some of these are displayed on the front porch on nicer days.

As West Pawlet grew larger and more prosperous (between 1880 and 1910 personal estates in the village quadrupled), the grumbling of its residents grew louder about having to go over the hill (although not nearly as steep as the one that separates the two parts of Dorset) to the town meetings. For years they had agitated to have them held in West Pawlet in alternating years, but were always outvoted by the residents of the eastern village.

Not only were there more residents in the main village, but living in closer proximity to the meeting place, they were more likely to get there to vote. And when there was any doubt, a boy was sent out in a buggy pulled by a fast Morgan mare named Fanny with a list of voters he was to round up and deliver to the town meeting.

The location of the town meeting each year created more problems than the one of geography: for the first few years the meetings were held at local taverns, of which there were enough to give a fair variety. In 1782, the residents voted to build a town house that could be used as a meeting hall and a place of worship. By 1818 it needed repairing, and the town voted instead to meet at each of the various churches in turn. They did this for 63 years.

By 1881, the town records needed a permanent home. But building a town hall of sufficient size was expensive. A most unusual plan was devised. Marcellus and Julia Wheeler owned a piece of land in the village center, which they sold to the town. They agreed to build the first story of a building of an agreed size, where they would operate their store. The town would build the second story, which would be large enough for citizen meetings and town offices. The contract spelled out in detail exactly who would build what.

The present town hall was built in 1881, with the store on its first floor, and that seemed to put an end to questions about where the town meeting would be held. But during the

Pawlet Town Hall

height of slate quarrying, West Pawlet was considerably more prosperous than Pawlet and continued to chafe under the irritating necessity of going seven miles over the hill to do business with the town.

In 1906, a group of West Pawlet citizens petitioned the legislature to form a separate town. The attempt failed, but left rancor behind it—so bitter that when one resident died and left his estate to the town, he stipulated that should the town ever be divided, not a penny of his bequest should go to the new town to the west.

In later years, the townspeople softened a bit, and voted to hold the meeting in the West Pawlet School every third year. These meetings were much rowdier affairs, not because the residents there were different, but because the school was within walking distance of the New York border. Vermont law prohibited all liquor sales on town meeting day (which was uniform throughout the state), but Pecue's Bar stood in

New York, barely over the line. Their business boomed that day, and the reverberations were heard later in the West Pawlet School, as debate grew heated, warmed in part by spirits other than town spirit.

A little booklet written at the celebration of the 100th anniversary of the "new" town hall comments that, "Although every effort is made to include both sides of Pawlet as 'one whole,' an invisible line springs up from time to time." (This booklet, which includes charmingly candid accounts of events in the town's history, as well as old photographs, is for sale at Mach's General Store.)

The core of Pawlet village still looks much as it did at the middle of the 19th century, except for the depot next to the store. While at first glance the depot may look perfectly at home in the center of a small town, a second look reveals that it overhangs a ravine and that there is no place where tracks could have gone. It was actually built in 1905 in Wallingford, Vermont, and after it fell to disuse, it was disassembled and moved here. It is now a restaurant where patrons have lunch at the counter or seated on old cast-iron and wooden slat benches.

Pottery artist Marion Waldo McChesney has her studio and salesroom on the ground floor of the brick house opposite Mach's, and Georganna Alexopoulos sells her exuberant hand-painted pottery from one of the old porched buildings across Route 30. The mill wheel at the dam across the street has been restored, and from the bridge, you get a good view of the narrow gorge worn by Flower Brook.

An even more dramatic view is from inside Mach's General Store, whose back room bridges the chasm. Amid the tin bins of nails, the mouse traps, flannel shirts, rubber boots, pickaxes, and push brooms, you'll see what appears to be a wooden cabinet, about elbow high. If you look down through its glass top, you'll get a direct-down view of the gorge and falls. There is nothing "Ye Olde Gifte Shoppe" about

Mach's. It is there to serve the community, and if it happens to have what a tourist is looking for, they're glad to sell it. It's hard to imagine anything one could want that isn't somewhere in the store. Next to the store, the newer Mach's Brick Oven Bakery serves lunch and snacks. Mach's has replaced the taverns (which are now, sadly, gone) as the center of the community. If you want to know what's happening, just listen, and read the posters and notices in the window.

Come November, one of the posters will be for the Pawlet Fire Station's Game Supper. Other Vermont towns have game suppers, but Pawlet's is the best. (That's not just our opinion; ask anybody standing in line.) It is always on the opening day of deer season, and people begin gathering at the fire station on Route 133 about 4:30 P.M. At the front of the line are Gordie and Phyllis Smith, who come over the border from New York every year to be the first to dip into the pot roast of bear, squirrel pie, moose meatballs, and venison sausage. Gordie and Phyllis have been coming for years, as have most of the other people waiting in line.

By the time the doors open, close to a hundred hungry, cold, and sometimes wet people stretch in a line across the front of the fire station and down the road. Kids, grandparents, seventh generationers, and the people from Connecticut who just retired to Dorset—it's as fine a mix of Vermonters as you'll find—missing only the New Agers, who are mostly vegetarians. Occasionally a car will drive right up to the front and a person will hop out carrying a big pan clutched in pot holders. Everyone makes way, and strains for a sniff of the contents. Dinner costs under 10 dollars, and your plate will be heaped with so many meats that you'll have trouble remembering which was the bear and which the moose. After that come the homemade pies.

Pawlet is still a town where people pitch in and help, newcomers and old-timers alike. The place buzzes with volunteers filling your coffee cup, replacing empty salad bowls, and bringing your pie. Is anybody there from West Pawlet? Of course; they know a bargain on a good meal. Their own fire station raises money by selling grinders to hunters. They'll even deliver, but presumably you have to come out of the woods and meet them at the road.

Places to See, Eat, and Stay

Mach's General Store, Pawlet 05775; (802) 325-3405. Open Monday through Saturday 7:00 A.M. to 6:30 P.M., Sunday 8:00 A.M. to 12:30 P.M.

Mach's Brick Oven Bakery, Pawlet 05775; (802) 325-6331. Serves lunch and snacks, and sells fresh-baked breads and pastries.

The Station Restaurant, Pawlet 05775; (802) 325-3041. A restaurant and lunch counter, open every day serving three meals in a railway station atmosphere.

Marion Waldo McChesney, Potter, Pawlet 05775; (802) 325-3100.

Georganna Alexopoulos, Hand Painted Pottery, RR 1, Box 2675, Pawlet 05761; (802) 325-3807.

3

VERGENNES:
THE INLAND TOWN
THAT GAVE BIRTH
TO A NAVY

(VERGENNES IS LOCATED WEST OF ROUTE 7,
19 MILES SOUTH OF BURLINGTON. IT CAN ALSO BE
REACHED VIA ROUTE 22A FROM THE SOUTH.)

When Vermont's only name was "the wilderness," Lake Champlain already bore the name of its discoverer, Samuel de Champlain, and it was the front line in a war between the North American empires of France and Great Britain. Champlain was told by his Indian guides that these hills on the eastern shore of the lake were inhabited by the Iroquois. Others have claimed that they were occupied by the Abenaki, but it is fairly certain that neither had a settlement here and that both used it as a hunting ground.

During the French and Indian Wars, from 1689 to 1763, Lake Champlain and the rivers joining it from the east became highways of war. Armed parties of French and Indi-

ans from Montreal and hostage-seeking bands from
the settlement of Saint Francis followed these
streams to their headwaters, crossing the
Green Mountains and then following
the rivers on the other side to the
Connecticut River to raid English settlements. Otter Creek was one of the primary
routes, its path running from the lake at Kellogg Bay in Ferrisburgh, through Middlebury and on to Dorset. From Otter
Creek it was a short portage over the mountains to the West
River and the Connecticut.

Although Benning Wentworth, Royal Governor of New
Hampshire, made a grant in 1761, it wasn't until that war
was over that settlement on the west side of the mountains
became safe. In 1766, sixteen young men from Salisbury,
Connecticut, traveled up the Connecticut River, then worked
their way through the forest until they came to Otter Creek
in Proctor. From there they floated down the creek to the
falls at the future Vergennes, cleared land, and set up their
farms and a sawmill. Within a few years, these few settlers at
the First Falls of Otter Creek, as it was then called, were dis-
possessed by another group, under a New York grant to
Colonel John Reid. Among his men was John McIntosh, a
veteran of Bonnie Prince Charlie's Battle of Culloden and
Wolfe's campaign at Quebec.

In the summer of 1772 Ethan Allen and a few of his
Green Mountain Boys happened to be in the area looking for
a New York surveyor when they found out what Reid and his
men had done. Immediately Allen's band removed Reid,
McIntosh, and the other New York claimants and restored
the property to the original New Hampshire grant settlers,
breaking the grindstones of a gristmill that Reid had
installed. Reid, a Scotsman and veteran of the Royal Highland Regiment, returned the following summer with a group
of newly arrived Scottish immigrants and again threw out

the original party. The Scots took over their houses and farms, and Reid banded the pieces of the grindstone together and again began operating his mill.

Ethan Allen's brother Ira soon came upon the settlement and, discovering what had happened, reported to Ethan. Gathering another group of 60 Green Mountain Boys, Ethan Allen and Seth Warner set out for the First Falls of Otter Creek and were joined by Remember Baker and his men. Forcing the Scots to remove their possessions from the houses, they burned six houses and the gristmill, and broke the grindstone into small pieces and threw it into the river. John McIntosh may have considered their offer of land in exchange for a pledge of loyalty to the New Hampshire grant holders, however, for his house was saved. Reid, who was away at the time of the raid, didn't reclaim his grant, and the gristmill war came to an end.

The settlement at the First Falls prospered because of the abundant power provided by the falls and the easy access Otter Creek provided to Lake Champlain. Iron ore was discovered in nearby Monkton, and furnaces were set up at the falls.

The only problem was that the growing community was located at the point where the towns of Panton, Waltham, and Ferrisburgh came together, and three different governments were directing their future. They petitioned the state, and in 1788 were granted a charter for a city (not a town) one and a half miles square with the falls at its core. In honor of the French foreign minister who negotiated the Treaty of Paris (which ended the French and Indian War), they named it Vergennes. This early date makes it the third oldest city in the United States, and its tiny dimensions put it among the smallest in the world.

The best place to see the falls is from McDonough Drive, which runs along a high terrace overlooking McDonough Harbor below. You can find it on the downhill side of Main

Street, just below Bixby Library. Even though the falls have been somewhat changed to increase their head, it is easy to see why their tremendous stores of energy attracted people to this site. Below the falls is a natural harbor, which even quite recently had a marina with berths for the many large sailing and motor vessels that use Otter Creek for access to Lake Champlain, only seven miles away.

It is this harbor that gives the tiny city of Vergennes its place in history. During the War of 1812 the lake had again become a major battleground. The British built a fleet in the Richelieu River at the north end of the lake that, by 1814, numbered 16 vessels, including the 37-gun *Confiance*. By the end of 1813, the small American fleet under Lieutenant Thomas McDonough was reduced to only three battered vessels as he sailed up Otter Creek to a winter port. Control of the lake was at issue, and with it the potential for control of northern New England.

While his fleet anchored just north of Dead Creek, McDonough continued up Otter Creek to Vergennes and began the building of his new fleet in the harbor at the foot of the falls. Within eight and a half months he built the 26-gun *Saratoga*, the 16-gun *Ticonderoga*, a 20-gun brig, three sloops, and eleven 75-foot gunboats, giving him a fleet of 17 new vessels to contest domination of the lake. All of the wood for *Saratoga* was cut within five and a half days and she was afloat in the incredible span of 40 days from the time her timbers were growing in the forest.

The site was a perfect one. McDonough had a harbor that was safe from attack by the British fleet, and the settlement at Vergennes offered not only sawmills for his lumber, but iron furnaces and blacksmith shops as well. Enough iron was produced from the ore of Monkton to make 177 tons of cannonballs for the fleet as well as much of the ironwork needed for the ships.

A look at a map shows that control of Otter Creek, and thereby the fleet, lay in the low-lying sandy spit of land now called Cassin Point. McDonough had a fort built on the point and put it under the command of Navy Lieutenant Cassin and Artillery Captain Thornton. He also had a secret narrow canal dug through the swamp to give him an alternative entrance to the lake.

On the 10th of May, the British attacked the little fort at the mouth of Otter Creek. After an all-day battle, the sound of which frightened everyone within miles, the British fleet withdrew, allowing McDonough and his entire fleet to enter the lake on May 11, 1814. After skirmishing all summer, the two fleets fought the last battle ever waged on Lake Champlain on October 11 at Plattsburgh, New York. McDonough's little hastily built fleet, still oozing sap from its timbers, had defeated the British. British troops withdrew to Canada, and a final peace fell on the Champlain Valley.

Nowhere in Vermont, for all the state's rich associations with the Revolution and the War of 1812, is there a place where we've stood with such an overwhelming sense of "this is where it all happened" as in Vergennes, looking down at that basin below the falls, knowing that the fleet that secured New England to the new United States was built right there.

If you follow McDonough Drive, it turns into Sand Road, and about six miles from Vergennes, Fort Cassin Road takes off to the left. While you can't go all the way to Fort Cassin (the whole point is privately owned and posted), you can get to the west end of Otter Creek, where you can envision the fleet sailing out into the lake. There's parking and a boat put-in along the banks, which are popular for fishing.

Marina services are now closer to the lake, about halfway between the falls and the mouth of Otter Creek, on Basin Harbor Road. Tom's Marine Service is set on a century-old riverside farm, with its barns still intact, and they offer berths and facilities for all boats, from kayaks and canoes to yachts. To reach Tom's, go south on Route 22A from the center of Vergennes and take Panton Road to the right, a short distance south of the river. After about a mile, Basin Harbor Road will diverge to the right.

Continue on this road to Basin Harbor for the Lake Champlain Maritime Museum, dedicated to teaching and preserving the maritime history of the lake from its earliest human use. It has dozens of original small watercraft built around the lake during the past 150 years, including a 54-foot replica of the *Philadelphia*, one of Benedict Arnold's ships from the naval battles of the lake during the Revolution. Exhibits detail both the naval history of the lake and its nautical archaeology; interactive exhibits allow children to learn such things as how pulleys helped people sail ships.

Using their collection of old wooden boats as inspiration, the museum also conducts boat-building courses and workshops for those who want to learn how to build their own wooden boat. A blacksmith forges ship parts in his authentic forge, and you can board the *Philadelphia*, which floats at dockside when it is not sailing in the lake. Nearby Button Bay State Park has nature programs, trails, and a small museum. You can also rent boats there, picnic, and hike along the shore and rocky ledges of the bay.

With naval battles during two wars and thousands of commercial and private vessels having sailed it, Lake Champlain has abundant underwater nautical sites that the maritime museum is trying to locate, survey, and protect. If you like to dive on shipwrecks, contact the Vermont Division for Historic Preservation for information on the Underwater Historic Preserve in Burlington Bay and off Colchester Point. A coal barge and another ship, the *General Butler*, are in Burlington Bay, and the *Phoenix I*, a steamer built in Vergennes in 1814 and sunk in 1819, is on the Colchester Shoal.

When, after the War of 1812, the Champlain Canal was completed, connecting the lake to the Hudson River, a new era of prosperity began in Vergennes and along the entire lake. Before that, most trade was with Canada, along the water routes to the north. During the 1830s and '40s a vast new market was opened to the cities in the south and west, which were growing with the new westward waves of settlement. The snug little harbor of Vergennes became a shipyard for the lake steamers and ferries that carried even more hill farmers giving up on their marginal farms to settle in the west. The banks of Otter Creek were bordered by a towpath for barges traveling to and fro with the products of the farmers who stayed.

The continuing prosperity of the town in the late 19th and early 20th centuries shows in the town hall, built in 1896, and the Bixby Library. The opera house is on the second floor of the city hall, and there are ambitious plans to keep its performance hall busy after the restorations are completed. The Bixby Memorial Free Library, a two-story brick Greek Revival building, was built in 1912. On the mezzanine and second floor, the library houses an extensive collection of Indian artifacts, the works of Vermont artists, and artifacts from the town's history.

Vergennes has somehow managed to keep a harmonious downtown district, retaining its graceful older buildings and avoiding discordant modern ones. There are over 80 homes and other structures in town that were built between 1800 and 1900, including some outstanding examples of commercial architecture in the downtown area around the park.

Downtown is no dusty museum but a lively place, its historic buildings in active use. A good example is the large old inn known as Stevens House, on the corner of Main and

Green Streets, which still has the two-story porches that overlook the street on the front and north side. Built in 1794, it served travelers until about 1970. It was restored as a bicentennial project in 1976 and now is a business block. In the rear of the renovated building is one of the area's three excellent French restaurants, Christophe's, serving a stylish, very French menu.

Also upscale, the Main Street Bistro serves dinners with a French flair in its intimate quarters in a business block south of the park. The third, Roland's Place, south of town on Route 7, is among Vermont's finest restaurants. French-born Roland serves an ambitious menu based on fresh local produce and meats from local specialty farms. Lunches and early-bird dinners are a real bargain.

For a quick meal we like Togo's Pizza, in the middle of town, with a good variety of pizza, plus sandwiches, pasta, and burgers. While the decor is definitely not upscale, Togo's has a wonderful display about the old opera house, including playbills from performances decades ago, photographs, and the story of the restoration, which was an example of the grassroots efforts that hold small towns together.

Vergennes is small enough to tour on foot, which gives you time to enjoy the diversity of the many Victorian homes that line the streets. While some have been converted to business uses, others are still private homes. One mansard-roofed Victorian home on Main Street that has been taking in guests for decades still offers year-round lodging. Emerson's Bed and Breakfast is a warm and comfortable B&B, furnished with antiques and collectibles. But you shouldn't get the idea that this is a museumlike establishment. The rooms are comfortably furnished and quiet, with both shared and private bath options. The full breakfast is served family-style around the large mahogany dining room table. Like every place in this compact town, Emerson's is only a short walk to the park and the center of town.

On the south end of Main Street, Strong House Inn has eight guest rooms, all with private baths, in a restored 1834 Federal-style house. The proprietors don't run south for the winter, either, but help their guests revel in the season by providing snowshoes, sleds, and toboggans to use on the property's hills and trails. Or you can bring your own skates to use on their rink. Those who prefer their winter activities indoors can join one of the inn's quilting programs, for three days of intensive quilt making.

Heading north on Route 22A, the Kennedy Brothers Factory Marketplace fills a converted factory building. It features a multidealer antiques center, a crafts area with a large number of crafts on display, the Kennedy Brothers Woodenware Factory Outlet, Ben & Jerry's, and other shops.

Three miles north on Route 7, the Rokeby Museum is the home of one of Vermont's earliest historians, Rowland Robinson, and a farm that was occupied by the Robinson family from 1780 until 1962. It was one of the primary stops on the Underground Railroad, and the secret room where runaway slaves were hidden is open to visitors. During the mid- and late 19th century, Robinson gathered the tales of the founding of Vermont, many from the mouths of the settlers or their children. He spent almost his entire life within the borders of the state, and his writings, although they sometimes reflect popular biases of the time, create a vivid picture of the birth and growing pains of the republic and the state.

Places to See, Eat, and Stay

Main Street Bistro, Main St., Vergennes 05491; (802) 877-3288. Fine dining with a French accent, serving dinner year-round Monday through Saturday.

Christophe's, Green St., Vergennes 05491; (802) 877-3413.

French food by a New York City chef who only opens this restaurant in the summer.

Roland's Place, Route 7 South, Vergennes 05491; (802) 453-6309. French cuisine using locally grown products in a beautifully restored historic tavern.

Togo's Pizza, Main St., Vergennes 05491. Sandwiches, pizza, burgers, pasta dishes, soups, and salads.

Emerson's Bed and Breakfast, 82 Main St., Vergennes 05491; (802) 877-3293. A bed-and-breakfast in a comfortable home.

Strong House Inn, Main St., Vergennes 05491; (802) 877-3337. A bed-and-breakfast in a Federal home.

Kennedy Brothers Factory Marketplace, Route 22A, Vergennes 05941; (802) 877-2975. Shops, an antiques market, and food.

Lake Champlain Maritime Museum, RR 3, Box 4092, Vergennes 05491; (802) 475-2317.

Underwater Historic Preserve, Division for Historic Preservation, Pavilion Building, Montpelier 05602; (802) 828-3226.

Rokeby Museum, Route 7, Ferrisburgh 05456; (802) 877-3406. Open May 1 through October 31, Thursday through Sunday, 10:30 A.M. to 3 P.M. (partially handicapped accessible).

Bixby Memorial Free Library, 258 Main St., Vergennes 05491; (802) 877-2211. Open Monday and Friday 12:30 to 8 P.M., Wednesday 10 A.M. to 5 P.M., Tuesday and Thursday 12:30 to 5 P.M. Vermontiana, Indian artifacts, works of Vermont artists, maps.

Town hall and opera house, Main St., Vergennes 05491; (802) 877-3637.

4

WINDSOR:
BUILT WITH
INTERCHANGEABLE
PARTS

(WINDSOR IS LOCATED ON U.S. ROUTE 5,
CLOSE TO INTERSTATE 91, 14 MILES SOUTH OF
WHITE RIVER JUNCTION.)

The west bank of the Connecticut River forms the east boundary of Windsor and provides a setting for the gutsy town that overlooks it from a narrow terrace and rolling hillsides. The river has been both friend and foe. In the early days it provided Windsor with a broad, easy highway to get goods to and from Connecticut and the settlements of western Massachusetts. But it also brought the periodic devastation of its floodwaters.

A century and a quarter after the *Mayflower* landed at Plymouth, this was still an uncharted wilderness between the sparse New Hampshire settlements to the east and those of New York across the mountains to the west. Both states laid

claim to these lands, but on July 6, 1761, New
Hampshire's Governor Wentworth issued a grant
of the town and got a jump on the "Yorkers."

The first settlers came up the river in 1764, and
by 1765 there were 15 people in town. Wary of
the problems caused in other towns by the bitter conflicting claims of the two royal
provinces, the citizens of Windsor, in 1772,

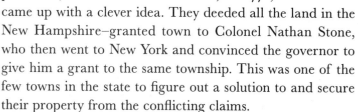

came up with a clever idea. They deeded all the land in the
New Hampshire–granted town to Colonel Nathan Stone,
who then went to New York and convinced the governor to
give him a grant to the same township. This was one of the
few towns in the state to figure out a solution to and secure
their property from the conflicting claims.

The measures New York was using to enforce its claim
throughout the surrounding territory led the people of all
these towns to send representatives to the Dorset Conventions to lay plans for establishing their own government. In
July 1777 they met again in Windsor. Although the settlers
had applied for admission to the fledgling United States in
1776, they had been refused because the Continental Congress feared upsetting the governments of the two claimant
states. In view of Congressional indecision (not a new problem, evidently), the delegates to the Windsor Convention
declared themselves to be the Republic of Vermont on July
8, 1777, at a meeting in the Elijah West Tavern.

While the convention was in session, word came that General Burgoyne's British troops had invaded along the Champlain valley and that Fort Ticonderoga had fallen. But a
sudden violent storm prevented the delegates from returning immediately to their threatened homes, so they settled in
and finished the work of setting up their republic.

The Old Constitution House, as the tavern is now called,
was only five years old at the time of the convention, and it
sat in the center of town, just west of where the old railroad

station now stands. In 1914 it was saved from its derelict state and moved to its present location on the northern end of Main Street, where it was preserved as a museum of the founding of Vermont. It has extensive displays on the history of the state and town; Old Constitution House is impressive both for its history and the fact that the town was only 10 years from the wilderness when it was built.

In the mid-19th century, any New England town with a sizable stream had a head start on prosperity, and Windsor had the fast-flowing Mill Brook, which was dammed to create Mill Pond. At first Windsor's citizens looked to the stream to power sawmills and gristmills, but as time passed, they developed bigger industries, which brought their community fame as the birthplace of the "American System" of manufacturing.

The gristmill, opened in Windsor in 1786 by Oliver Adams, was among the first to be genuinely automated. It was powered by a waterwheel that operated not only the grindstone but leather belts with small tin scoops attached. In early mills the grain was poured into a funnel, ground by the stones, and then spilled out onto the floor, where it was swept up (along with whatever had been tracked in on workmen's boots) before being shoveled into bags and barrels. In this new-style mill, the grain was released from large storage bins and was ground into flour. It fell into collection devices from which the scoops carried it to the upper floors, where it was bagged or put into barrels.

An archaeological dig of the foundations of the mill has uncovered artifacts including one of the original scoops that carried the flour. You can see the mill site from the bridge over South Main Street on the northern side of Mill Brook, and the artifacts are in the American Precision Museum, where there is also a model of the mill that shows exactly how it worked. The beautifully detailed model is worth seeing even if you're not interested in mills—it's art.

The historic red mill building that houses the American Precision Museum is itself a classic example of an early industrial age waterpowered factory. It sits on a small gorge and waterfall that was dammed to provide even more head to power its machinery. The American Precision Museum houses displays and the actual machinery and tools that changed the way things were manufactured and made our modern world possible.

Before the Industrial Revolution every object had to be made by a craftsman, one at a time. Each was unique and there were no interchangeable parts, so that if, for example, a gun barrel were damaged, a whole new gun had to be made by a gunsmith. In Windsor, and in a few other small towns around New England, people began to think about and develop systems for manufacturing objects with parts that would fit others. This was the birth of the concept of interchangeable parts. The secret to this so-called "American System" of manufacturing was machines that could shape and mill individual parts so precisely that each was identical to the other.

In 1800 Asahel Hubbard came to Windsor and became one of its leading citizens and pioneer industrialists. In 1828 he patented the hydraulic pump and began manufacturing them the following year. He managed to have himself appointed warden of the state prison at Windsor and set up his shop in the prison, which provided him a ready and cheap source of labor at the rate of 25 cents a day. The pumps were an immediate success and were sold across the country and abroad. The story is told that after he had installed a new pump for the St. Louis, Missouri, water company and found that they were unable to pay for it, he accepted a white horse in barter and rode it all the way back to Windsor.

In 1835 Hubbard begin manufacturing guns based on a design by his son-in-law, the gunsmith Nicanor Kendall.

Kendall is said to have designed the new gun after his accidentally misfired, injuring his own hand and parting the hair of his betrothed (the daughter of his boss, Asahel Hubbard) while they were out hunting. The first big sale for the company's new gun was to the Republic of Texas, which paid for them by deeding over two thousand acres of land.

Richard Smith Lawrence moved to town in 1838 and went to work for Kendall, who by that time had taken over the Hubbard business. By 1846 Lawrence was a partner in the Robbins and Lawrence Armory and Machine Shop, which opened its new factory that year. It was the most modern arms factory in the world, based upon the new principle of precision manufacturing. In 1851 the firm's rifles were exhibited in England, and the British were so impressed that the government bought the company's machine tools to retool the Royal Armory at Enfield. When, in 1855, Great Britain was engaged in the Crimean War, an order was placed for another twenty-five thousand guns. That is how the small town of Windsor gave birth to the famed British "Enfield" rifle that won England an empire.

In 1858, Vermont Arms Company, which had taken over Robbins and Lawrence, also began making sewing machines based on the designs of the Reverend John A. Dodge, another Windsor inventor. Later that part of the business was sold off and became the White Sewing Machine Company. The demands of the American Civil War further added to the success of the company.

After the Civil War, the demand for guns dropped and the Robbins and Lawrence Armory was converted to making tools and goods for civilian use. By 1870 it had become a cotton factory, and from 1898 to 1966 it served as a hydroelectric generating plant. With such a long and varied career, it's an appropriate home for the American Precision Museum.

The museum's exhibits are divided into three parts. The first shows the principles of precision manufacturing techniques and the tools used in the process. The displays incorporate products made in that building to show the importance of the site. The second section shows the importance of precise measurement and testing, using hands-on displays. The third focuses on the number of different machines and skills required in these plants, using photographs dating from the 1850s.

The Machine Tool Hall of Fame, which fills an immense shop area, has an impressively large collection of historic machines, tools, and parts that really bring the museum alive. Two intricate operating scale models of turn-of-the-century machine shops, together with a scale model of an early steam-powered generating plant, are fascinating. The importance of the museum was recognized by the American Society of Mechanical Engineers when they made it their first International Mechanical Engineering Heritage Site in 1987.

After the conversion of the plant in 1870, a group of its employees formed the Windsor Machine Company, continuing the town's role in the development of machine tools. Another of Windsor's fledgling tool and die making industries, the Jones and Lamson Company, was acquired by a group of men from Springfield, Vermont, in 1888. Under the leadership of James Hartness that company became one of the premier machine tool manufacturers in the United States. The tradition of machine tool manufacture still continues with the Cone-Blanchard Company, although on a diminished scale. During World War II, over 20 percent of all the machine tools made to produce American war matériel were manufactured in Windsor and nearby Springfield.

The presence of all of this industry guaranteed that Windsor would be a main stop when the railroad was extended up the Connecticut River. The grand Victorian station, built in 1900 to handle the passengers and freight that passed through, still stands on Depot Avenue, downhill from Main Street. It's now a restaurant, serving meals in the restored wood-paneled waiting area of the station. Across the street its Deli and Bakery offers breakfast, sandwiches, pastry, and picnic makings. Their sandwiches are made on their own fresh-baked bread, and they offer a box lunch with sandwich, chips, fresh-baked cookie, and fruit drink for $6.25.

The profits of Windsor's manufacturing meant that it could afford to indulge in fine public buildings and residences. From 1800 to 1804, the American architect Asher Benjamin lived and worked in Windsor and adorned the town and area with his buildings. A follower of Charles Bulfinch, he operated a school of architecture in town for five years. He had a great influence on building design throughout the United States because his several books were widely used by carpenters and architects of the period. The Old South Congregational Church, on the west side of Main Street opposite the municipal building, is believed to have been designed by him and incorporates many of his design features. In the mid-1980s an architectural model was built following his 1803 plans for a house in Randolph Center, Vermont. This detailed model is on display at the Windsor House, which we'll get to shortly.

The buildings of Windsor are not confined to the early 19th century. Examples of many other styles stand along Main Street, State Street, and the side streets. Some of the best examples are the outstanding Gothic Revival houses at 5 Court Street and 35 North Main Street, the Italianate granite post office and federal courthouse, and the Richardsonian Romanesque town hall.

While manufacturing riches built this fine, stylish town, the financial hard times that came after the decline of the machine tool industry probably saved this architectural heritage. As one resident told us, "Windsor's architecture was never ruined because no one had the money to 'improve' it." This silver-lining legacy of hard times has also left Windsor with a central business district that reflects the best of the late 19th century, including a brick gable-ended Georgian block and the stone Tracy and Tuxbury blocks. The columns on the Tuxbury block are cast iron, and its Roman Revival facade has corbeling and arched windows. The Tracy block is a classic Italianate commercial structure.

The best way to appreciate the architectural riches of Windsor is to walk its streets following either or both of the suggested walking tours prepared by Historic Windsor. A detailed map describes over 60 buildings. It can be obtained at the Windsor House, which is itself one of the town's most striking buildings.

The two-story columned porches of the Windsor House have graced Main Street since the building was erected in 1840, on the site of the tavern where Lafayette had greeted townspeople during his grand tour of New England in 1825. Well into the 20th century it was considered to be one of the most outstanding hotels north of Boston. Closed in the 1960s, it was scheduled for destruction but saved at the last minute in 1972 by the concerted effort of people who recognized its importance as the focal point of Main Street. Its exterior restored, the interior is now one of the two main showrooms of the Vermont State Craft Center, featuring the handworks of noted Vermont craftspeople in many media. It also houses Historic Windsor, the Asher Benjamin model, and a large rack of travel information.

Windsor's connection to its sister towns across the river in New Hampshire is illustrated by a painting on the wall of the Vermont National Bank on Main Street. During the early decades of the 20th century, the artist Maxfield Parrish—whose home was in Cornish, New Hampshire—often came across the river to do his banking. Notoriously bad at balancing his account, he promised the tellers that if they would do it for him he would give them an oil painting. His 1942 painting *Thy Templed Hills* was duly delivered, and it is there today on the wall behind the tellers. It is understood that it belongs to them, not to the bank. Even now, the cross-river kinship of the Connecticut River towns shows in promotional brochures for Windsor and the mix of license plates along Main Street.

Maxfield Parrish was not the only Cornish Colony artist to spend time in Windsor. Sculptor Augustus Saint-Gaudens, novelist Winston Churchill, and many others came here for business and social life in homes on these hills. Windsor also had its own literary attractions. The publisher Maxwell Evarts Perkins of Charles Scribner's Sons discovered Ernest Hemingway, F. Scott Fitzgerald, and Thomas Wolfe, and edited works of many other of this century's greatest and best-known writers, many of whom visited him here. His grandfather, Senator William Maxwell Evarts, had assembled a compound of houses that his family continued to use and where Perkins spent his summers.

Senator Evarts was one of the leading men of mid-19th-century America. As Acting Attorney General of the United States, he successfully defended President Andrew Johnson from impeachment charges and later served as Secretary of State under Rutherford B. Hayes. It is ironic that his great-grandson, Archibald Cox, was fired as Watergate Special Prosecutor during the nation's only other impeachment proceedings, against President Richard Nixon.

In 1901 the senator's son, Maxwell, inherited three hundred acres when his father died, and he built a noble Georgian Revival–style home, which he named Juniper Hill Farm. Its Ionic-columned trellis is believed to have been modeled after a similar one on the home of Augustus Saint-Gaudens across the river in Cornish. The house remained in his family until it was turned into an inn in 1944 by Catherine "Kip" Cushman, the pioneering engineer who created the Mount Ascutney Ski Area. The meticulously maintained Juniper Hill Inn is run today by Rob and Susanne Pearl, whose welcome matches the grace of their inn.

High on a hill, it overlooks the town, the river, and Runnemede Pond below, and Mount Ascutney beyond. The two wings of the inn, featuring matching Palladian windows, flank the entry into the inn's enormous raised-wood-paneled parlor, which is reminiscent of the great hall of an English manor house, except for the large windows that fill it with light. Juniper Hill serves a full breakfast (which you can order delivered to your room), as well as dinners, well prepared and nicely presented on fine china and crystal stemware. Reservations are essential for dinner in the candlelit dining room, where there is one seating at 7 P.M. daily. Close by the inn are a waterfall and the trails of Paradise Park, which Rob or Susanne will be happy to tell you about.

Windsor is connected to New Hampshire by the longest covered bridge in the United States, at the end of Bridge Street, off the southern end of Main Street. On the left side of the street at number 45, just before the bridge, is the old toll house, built about 1797. The first bridge was built in 1796, replacing a ford that soaked one of the area's earliest preachers every Sunday when he came across from his parish in New Hampshire for services. He held Windsor services in the homes of his flock, and they didn't really like him dripping all over their floors. The present bridge was built in 1866, the fourth in this spot, and was a toll bridge until 1953.

During the past several decades, Windsor's machine tool industry lost its place in the market, and businesses have closed or been forced to cut back. The Goodyear plant, which for years had provided a reliable employment base, pulled out of town in the early 1980s, and the snowless winters later in that decade led to the closing of the Mount Ascutney Ski Area and its associated businesses. A hard-working blue-collar town all of its life, Windsor found itself with rising assistance rolls. Even those with jobs had to apply the bittersweet adage "Moonlight in Vermont—or Starve."

Throughout the years, however, the self-reliant spirit that guided the valley settlers has kept the town going and has maintained its hope. Historic Windsor, founded to save the Windsor House, has broadened its goals and serves as a driving force to restore the downtown area. It conducts annual workshops of the Preservation Institute for the Building Crafts, teaching all aspects of the art of antique building restoration. Ascutney Mountain has reopened, and it thrives as a family-oriented ski and winter sports resort.

Windsor's solid work ethic and the treasures of its architectural past have begun to attract professional people as residents. Newcomers quickly learn that they can't just move in and tell people what they're doing wrong, nor can they demand instant respect, but if they show a willingness to pitch in, and if they treat people with respect, they will be accepted without reservation. But as one newcomer said, laughing, while he surveyed a half-finished carpentry project, there are a few immutable truths newcomers do have to learn; for example, come deer season they shouldn't plan to get anything done for at least two weeks.

Places to See, Eat, and Stay

Windsor Station Restaurant, Depot Square, Windsor 05089; (802) 674-2052. Deli and Bakery; (802) 674-2675.

Juniper Hill Inn, Juniper Hill Rd., RR 1, Box 79, Windsor 05089; (802) 674-5273 or (800) 359-2541.

Old Constitution House, North Main St., Windsor 05089; (802) 672-3773. Open Memorial Day through Columbus Day, daily 10 A.M. to 5 P.M.

American Precision Museum, 196 Main St., P.O. Box 679, Windsor 05089; (802) 674-5781. Open May 20 through November 1.

Vermont National Bank, 50 Main St., Windsor 05098; (802) 674-2131.

Vermont State Craft Center, Windsor House, Main St., Windsor 05098; (802) 674-6729 or (800) 376-6882. Open January through May, Monday through Friday 10 A.M. to 4 P.M., Saturday 10 A.M. to 3 P.M., and Sunday 11 A.M. to 3 P.M.; from May through December, Monday through Saturday 9:30 A.M. to 5:30 P.M., and Sunday 11:30 A.M. to 4:30 P.M.

Preservation Institute for the Building Crafts, Main St., P.O. Box 1777, Windsor 05098; (802) 674-6752.

Ascutney Mountain Resort, Route 44, Brownsville 05037; (802) 484-7711, reservations and snow conditions (800) 243-0011. Downhill and Nordic skiing, snowboarding, sports and fitness center, tennis.

North Star Canoe Livery, RR 2, Box 894, Cornish, NH 03745; (603) 542-5802. Canoe rentals, private transportation, shuttle service, raft trips (two-hour, day, and multiday trips), inn-to-inn canoeing trips. South on Route 12A, three miles from the New Hampshire end of the covered bridge.

Yankee Rambler Vacations: see Juniper Hill Inn. Packaged vacation trips that include canoe and/or bicycle rental, transportation to and from the rental site, route planning and lodging, and some meals at the Juniper Hill Inn.

Merry Wives of Windsor, Route 5 south of Windsor; (802) 674-5748. A gallery of art and 19th- and 20th-century furniture, glassware, bronzes, and antiques. Open mid-May through mid-December, Wednesday through Sunday, or by appointment.

5

BRANDON:
THE TOWN
THAT SURVIVED

(BRANDON IS ON U.S. ROUTE 7,
17 MILES NORTH OF RUTLAND.)

Walking down the broad, tree-shaded streets lined with well-kept 19th-century homes, you wouldn't characterize Brandon as a town that had kept up with the times. Little appears to have changed in the past hundred years. But the foresight of its residents and their ability to adapt quickly to change has kept the town vibrant, economically sound, and prosperous enough to maintain its outstanding architecture and its historic air. Brandon is a survivor.

Unlike so many of the towns in western Vermont, Brandon didn't offer its early settlers prime farmland. The rich alluvial soil so common in neighboring towns is found only in the limited area along Otter Creek; the rest of Brandon's base is on the sands of an ancient beach, a terrace of heavy clay good for growing grass, but not much else.

Of the five men who began clearing homesteads in the area in the summer of 1761, only the blacksmith, Amos Cutler, decided not to return home for the winter, staying alone there with his dog. The others rejoined him in the spring and became permanent settlers. It is oddly appropriate that the first permanent settler should be a blacksmith. For what nature didn't give Brandon in soil, it made up for in minerals, especially iron ore. In addition, the Neshobe River, which flows into Otter Creek in Brandon, although small, drops smartly over a falls, providing plenty of head to power mills. It is a New England quirk that the size of a body of water has little relation to its name, thus the smaller Neshobe River runs into the larger Otter Creek, already a sizable one, and Vermont's longest river, in fact. This probably results from the early practice of naming a stream at whatever point it was first encountered. Otter Creek may have been deemed a creek by early settlers in Dorset, where it rises as a small mountain brook.

The combination of iron ore and water power made Brandon an ideal site for iron manufacture, and the first furnace was operating at the falls (in the center of what is now the downtown commercial area) by 1788. By the turn of the century forges were added, and Brandon's iron business was underway.

It was a carpenter, however, who realized the full potential of iron and made Brandon an important iron-working center. In 1796 John Conant came to Brandon and, seeing the mills, the falls, and the iron works, bought the waterpower rights in the area of the village and established a small factory to make the simple hand tools every early household needed. As his business grew, he bought more water rights and opened new mills, soon expanding his tool business to the manufacture of iron stoves.

The Conant Stove was greeted enthusiastically by those who were used to cooking over a fireplace. It had a firebox, an oven, and an extended section on either side for warming. A large circular opening in the back allowed for a washtub and griddle. It was a big improvement from a pot hanging on a crane over an open fire. (If you should chance onto a Conant Stove at an auction, don't let it go without a fight.)

Another furnace was opened in the part of town called Forestdale, about four miles from the center of the village. By the middle of the 1840s, Royal Blake had built an entire little village surrounding his iron works there. Much of that village remains today, along Route 73 toward Brandon Gap. Workers' cottages, the office, a company store, and even the enormous furnace still stand. The furnace is nearly hidden in the woods below Route 73. Blake's own home, built of stone, stands on the hill above the furnace. Blake even built the little Episcopal chapel across the road from it.

Conant's furnace and forge were in the center of Brandon village. The building almost on top of the bridge, now used as town offices, with the pair of chimneys and the fanlight in its gable, was originally Conant's office building. If you walk west on the main street, past the monumental old town hall, you will pass Conant's home, a fine brick Federal on the corner of Prospect Street, opposite the Episcopal Church. The house was built in 1802, some years before the office building.

The wide street on which Conant's home faced is known as Conant Square, and the third of the three fine mid-19th-century buildings on the opposite side was originally a tavern built by Conant in 1818. With this he added tavern-keeping to his iron and construction businesses (he was a carpenter, remember). But in 1830, he joined the growing Temperance movement and became quite active. Of course he closed the tavern and turned his energies to supervising the building of the Baptist Church, just beyond, at the head of Crescent Park. He also paid for most of it.

The previous year, the Congregationalists had built their church on the other side of the river, within sight of the bridge, at a point where the stage road turned and went down the hill to the river crossing. Each church faced a separate green, so instead of the town growing around a single common area as most New England towns did, Brandon grew between the two. As this area filled, other roads leading from the village became residential streets, and these were connected by shorter ones.

Following the construction of the two churches and the establishment of the greens that face them, two new streets were laid out, Pearl and Park, each leading from the front of its respective church in a straight line. The streets themselves were wide, and the houses were set back from them so they could be used for parades or places for the local militia to march and conduct maneuvers.

As you try to "read" the history of Vermont towns by the evidence that remains today, look for these wide straight streets with all the houses set back to an even line. They were usually parade grounds for the militia. (One exception to this seems to be Church Street in Dorset. Although it certainly looks like a parade street, there is no evidence in the historical records that it was meant or ever used for one.)

Brandon's were used, by Allen's Greys, a militia company named for Ethan Allen. Written accounts of their annual Muster Day in early June ring with patriotic pride, and describe their blue coats, white trousers, and "bell-crowned leather helmets with tall white and red plumes." These two streets with their stately homes seem the perfect setting for a militia muster on a fine June day. These musters were attended by everyone, since nearly every man in town was a member and the women came to serve refreshments and watch the drills. When the Civil War came, Brandon, like

almost every other town in Vermont, sent more than its share
into the Union Army; Vermont had the highest proportion of
soldiers in relation to its population of any Union state. A
monument stands in the green at the head of Park Street
commemorating those who served.

Vermont, whose constitution has prohibited slavery since
its formation as a state, was a major force in the Underground Railroad. In fact, Vermont courts refused to restore
apprehended slaves to their "rightful" owners, despite federal law to the contrary. A number of routes for escaping
slaves ran the length of Vermont, and Brandon was a stop on
the main one in the western part of the state. The home of
attorney Rodney Marsh, an active abolitionist, is thought to
have been a stop on this road to freedom; it still stands on
Pearl Street, the large brick house with the columned portico.
A large hotel that stood by the railway tracks was also
reputed to have been a stop, and locals tell of sneaking in as
children to exploring its hidden underground tunnel to the
river.

Abolitionism ran so strong in Republican Brandon, and
in the rest of the state, that in the presidential election of
1860, the town (and state) supported Abraham Lincoln over
their own native son, Stephen A. Douglas. The latter, born
in a small house facing Brandon's Crescent Park, was an
influential U.S. senator who supported the right of new states
to allow slavery, a notion that found few supporters in his
native state. It certainly didn't help that when he was cam-
paigning in Brandon, which he had left to go west as a young
man, he observed in the course of his hour-long speech that
"Vermont is the most glorious spot on the face of the globe
for a man to be born in—provided he emigrates when he is
very young."

By the time the Civil War broke out, Brandon was already
a flourishing industrial center. The Rutland-Burlington Railroad had opened a line through town in 1849, making it eas-

ier to ship finished products to market. Brandon business-men soon realized the opportunities this link presented, and as the iron industry began to decline, others quickly replaced it. Railway cars were manufactured in a shop on Center Street. In 1857, in the machine shop of the old Brandon Iron Works, a new type of scale was developed. It became known as the Howe Scale, named for the Brandon man who pur-chased the rights to its manufacture, which continued here for 20 years.

Marble quarries opened, and with them developed two marble cutting and polishing plants. One of these quarries, on Route 7 north of town, is still in operation today, making fillers for paints and plastics. Ocher clay, which was a by-product of iron ore, became the basis for a thriving paint business. Kaolin was taken from the iron mines and made into tile.

The foresight to predict economic changes and act before they occurred, instead of reacting after them, helped to keep Brandon's economy thriving after the Civil War. Sawmills opened to process the yield of the many nearby lumbering operations. Other woodcraft industries and new marble plants opened, in a process of economic survival still at work today.

Meanwhile, the village grew into a busy trade center, with brick business blocks lining the area close to the falls. The largest of these, on the west side of Route 7, is decorated with ornate cast-iron work on its storefronts and marble over its upper windows. The turn of the century saw a prosper-ous town, with attractive public and private buildings, look-ing much as it does today.

Brandon's location and atmosphere appealed to summer people and travelers, in an age when travel was becoming popular. The Brandon Inn, whose fine brick facade faces the green and the Civil War monument, was built on the site of a former inn, attracting the carriage trade to its stylish guest and dining rooms. It carries its age well, and guests still enjoy relaxing in the rockers on the wide veranda and watching the town go by.

It was as a summer resident that Albert Farr, a wealthy banker, came to Brandon and built the most extravagant home in town on Park Street. It was state of the art in 1909, and the Farrs came every summer with their staff of 16 and their Pierce Arrow. The Arches became the year-round home of Shirley Farr, a dynamic and determined heiress who became one of the town's chief benefactors, as well as its representative to the state legislature. She also endowed the library and left the land for Branbury State Park.

After the stock market crash in 1929, which the Farr fortunes survived, she bought the mortgages on all the homes on Park Street, and saw to it that the buildings were kept up. All of her workmen lived on the street, and when she died, her will left them their houses. Yet she abhorred the sight of a lunch pail, so none of them dared carry one to work.

The Arches stayed in the Farr family until 1970, and is now owned by Melanie and Michael Shane. Melanie is an architect with special expertise in interior design, which shows clearly in her work of turning this Craftsman-period home into Lilac Inn. Their outstanding dining room (which extends onto a rear courtyard in the summer) is small, elegantly oak paneled, and serves lighter fare as well as full-course dinners. Guests still feel as though they're staying in a private summer estate.

Another summer resident who left a mark on Brandon was Henry Watson, a New Yorker who was among a small group of people who feared that the unique breed of Vermont horse, the Morgan, would die out entirely. By the turn of the 20th century, there had been so much cross-breeding that many of the horses called Morgans actually had little Morgan stock in them. Watson spent his summers at his Brandon farm, where he raised horses, among them Morgans. He and several others formed the Morgan Horse Club, predecessor of the Morgan Breeding Club, at the Vermont State Fair in 1907, offering prizes for the entrants most closely resembling the originals. This helped renew interest in the breed that had carried the Vermont cavalry into the Civil War; the club's work was largely responsible for preserving the Morgan.

Like the Farrs, Watson used his money for the benefit of the town and for many years not only hosted, but paid for, the Brandon Town Fair, held annually at his farm.

The first of Watson's farms later became the Brandon Training School, but he had several. The splendid barn at Edgeview Antique Rose Garden, on Marble Street, stabled Morgan stallions and brood mares. The barn has an elevator in it and now houses a small shop selling rose-related gifts and books.

The owners of Edgeview, Albert and Shirley Hill, have created an entire garden of antique rose varieties, many quite rare, and all of which date from before 1920. Separated by manicured grass pathways, the varieties are labeled, and your host will gladly tell you about particular roses or answer questions. Very few gardens like it exist anywhere, and you will see (and inhale the fragrances of) over two hundred kinds of roses, all common before the turn of the century, when hybridization became popular. From late May to October, there will be roses blooming, although they are at their peak between June 10 and July 10. Varieties range from the native pasture roses of New England to blossoms esteemed in 14th-century European gardens.

Brandon has several other places of interest to those who love flowers and herbs: Country Herbs and Flowers grows culinary and medicinal herbs in their display gardens, and

St. Thomas Church at Conant Square has a garden of plants mentioned in the Bible where visitors are welcome to stroll.

On Fridays from mid-June through mid-October, Brandon Farmer's Market is held in Central Park, in front of the Brandon Inn. Along with the produce of local gardens—fruits, vegetables, flowers, and herbs—you'll find maple syrup, baked goods, jams, and jellies.

While it is certainly not a "made for tourists" town full of cute boutiques, Brandon has a number of activities for visitors, including a busy schedule of musical performances at Lilac Inn and Friday evening performances by a folk singer in the Neshobe Tavern at the Brandon Inn. Behind the inn is the Vermont Ski Museum, with displays of more than seven hundred items showing the technology and history of the sport.

Although not as critical to Brandon's economy as some of the other treasures hidden in the ground beneath it, surely the most puzzling underground phenomenon is the frozen well. People refer to it obliquely, sometimes slyly, as when they mention the "frozen frog," as though they really don't expect you to believe it. Until we ran across a mention of it in a book published in the 1890s, we thought it was just another example of the finely honed Vermont sense of humor at work. But there it was, in the writing of a woman who had just devoted several pages to an admiring description of the local biblical scholar. We're not suggesting she swears this on a stack of Bibles, but she doesn't seem the sort to make up legends. So here goes. She says, and we quote:

> In the southwest part of town, not far from the village, is a frozen well, which, since 1858, the year of its accidental discovery, has excited the interest of such eminent scientists as Sir Charles Lyell, Professors [Louis] Agassiz, Jackson and others who have visited it. This well lies between two nearly parallel ridges of

limestone, which are about an eighth of a mile apart. It is forty feet deep, the water very clear, with pebbly bed. Ice forms in the well no later than April, but if not taken away remains usually through the summer, while the stones are coated with ice for four or five feet above water the mercury marking 1°F. above freezing. The phenomenon of this frozen well is thus explained in the latest geological reports: "The deposit is probably about the age of moraine terraces, whose peculiarities we have supposed produced by stranded icebergs, and that the gravel and sand among these were doubtless frozen . . . tens of thousands of years ago, but marly clay and pebbles is a poor conductor of heat. The conditions are like those of a huge sandstone refrigerator. . . ."

Now about the frozen frog story: you'll have to track that one down for yourselves.

Places to See, Eat, and Stay

Lilac Inn, 53 Park St., Brandon 05733; (802) 247-5463. Dinner and lunch served Wednesday through Saturday, brunch on Sunday. The menu changes weekly. Order your dessert of double chocolate crème brûlée at the beginning of your meal, since it needs to be specially prepared.

The Brandon Inn, On the Village Green, 20 Park St., Brandon 05733; (802) 247-5766. Known for its fine dining room, as well as comfortable lodgings.

Edgeview Antique Rose Garden, 27 Marble St., Brandon 05733; (802) 247-6095. Memorial Day through Columbus Day. Admission is $3.50, $3 for students and seniors, $8 for a family. Please call first for an appointment.

Country Herbs and Flowers, 57 Pearl St., Brandon 05733; (802) 247-3653. Open Tuesday through Saturday, 10 A.M. to 4 P.M. Admission free.

The Vermont Ski Museum, 20 Park St., Brandon 05733; (802) 247-8080. Open May through October. Admission $2, children over 12 50¢, seniors $1.50. Inquire at the Brandon Inn.

For more information on Brandon, contact the Brandon Area Chamber of Commerce, P.O. Box 267, Brandon 05733; (802) 247-6401. The information center is in the tiny white building opposite the Civil War monument.

6

MIDDLETOWN SPRINGS: THE TOWN THAT KEPT CHANGING ITS NAME

(MIDDLETOWN SPRINGS IS LOCATED ON ROUTE 133, 15 MILES SOUTHWEST OF RUTLAND.)

While Dorset and Pawlet made the best of their divided geographies, a group of settlers farther north took a different approach. They had chosen a protected valley along the upper Poultney River and had cleared the land, established farms, and even organized churches. The only problem with their valley community was that it sat squarely at the intersection of the boundaries of four towns. The rugged mountains surrounding them effectively cut these corners off from the main portion of each town.

They did the only sensible thing: petitioned the legislature for a new incorporation made up of corners of all four towns, with its borders running along the tops of the mountains. "Nature formed the territory for the town," an early historian observed, and the legislature simply recorded it. It may be the only town in Vermont that follows natural boundaries. The surveyor who drew the lines was given the honor of naming the new town. He couldn't find a more appropriate name than that of his former home, which was Middletown, Connecticut. The "Springs" came later.

In 1785, residents held their first town meeting and formally elected people to all the necessary jobs, from moderator and clerk to fence viewer, pound keeper, and leather sealer.

The settlement was isolated, but it was on the main stagecoach route between Rutland and Salem, New York. Parts of the old road are left, some too overgrown for travel except on foot; one of its milestone markers remains, built into a stone fence at the corner of Route 133 and Wells Road. Farming was the mainstay of the economy, but mills were built along the river, and stores and two taverns surrounded the green. A traveler in these early days didn't think much of the accommodations, however, noting tersely in his journal: "retched fare, retched bed, eat up with fleas, no hay, horse starving."

By 1811 gristmills and sawmills, a forge, foundry, distillery, carding mill, cider mill, tannery, and mill for producing linseed oil were operating on the power the Poultney supplied. One of the original stores, next to the Congregational Church, is now the historical society.

In July of 1811, after a day of torrential thunderstorms, the Poultney River rose so rapidly from the runoff of its mountain tributaries that nearly everything along the river was carried away. Mills, equipment, livestock, homes, and businesses were lost, along with several lives. One family, their house surrounded by the rising waters, was saved by the quick thinking of a man on the opposite bank, who suggested dragging the Liberty Pole from its place in a shed next to the church. Securing one end on the bank, they threw the other end upstream and let the waters carry it so that it lodged against the foundation on the other side, forming a precarious bridge across the swirling waters. With the bell-rope from the meetinghouse tied around his waist, he "climbed" the pole, which was partially under water, to the stranded house. He then lifted the end and wedged it into the front door, above the water level, and secured the rope so that all 14 of the occupants could steady themselves on it as they walked the pole to safety. Within 15 minutes, the house was swept away.

The flood changed the course of the river and buried in silt and stones a spring that had been used by the Indians before the valley was settled. But more of that later. By then the original builder of most of the mills, an old man dispirited by the destruction, rebuilt only the forge and sawmill. Middletown declined in importance as a center for industry. With jobs gone, residents began to move elsewhere and the population declined.

But a good water source was still an asset, bound to attract new industry. The only mills to survive the flood were owned by a relative of Albert W. Gray, who went to work there as a boy of 15. From the beginning he showed promise, and by the time he reached age 21, he was among the most respected workmen in the area. Old enough at last to go into business for himself, five years later he was granted his first patent, for a corn sheller.

In the early 19th century, all farmwork was done by hand, with the aid of animals for hauling loads or pulling plows. Each of the many steps, from plowing to preparing for storage, was labor- and time-intensive. Albert Gray began to change that when, in 1844, he patented a treadmill for horses. He continued to improve on its design until 1857, when he began to manufacture them in Middletown.

The principle sounded simple enough: a revolving platform of two-inch-thick maple planks, wide enough for one or two horses, set at a slant that would keep the animals moving continuously and steadily. Underneath the planks, wrought-iron cogs met those of a driveshaft connected to a belt that carried the power to the machine being operated. Until this invention, threshing grain was a long, slow, backbreaking job. Gray's first machine built to work with the treadmill was a thresher, to which he quickly added a separator and winnower. The machine delivered good clean grain directly to a measure, and thence to the bag.

It literally revolutionized farming, not just for the big operators, but for the family farm as well. Big farms bought stationary models to be attached to the floor of the threshing room. Small farmers hired the machine by the day from owners of carriage-mounted models, which traveled from farm to farm.

The treadmill factory soon became Middletown's major employer, with as many as one hundred workers. Although Gray's mill had access to waterpower on the Poultney River, he used his own treadmills to operate the smaller machinery in his shop, and sold models designed for use by small shop owners who had no, or an unreliable, water supply. Not surprisingly, the machines were shipped all over the world. Since Middletown was not on a railway line, the heavy machines had to be hauled by horsecart to the nearest station in Poultney, eight miles away.

Gray never stopped improving his designs, adding new features and creating new machines to work by horsepower. Silage cutters, drag and circular saws, and others continued to make farmwork more efficient. Not until the development of the internal combustion engine and the rise of big farm machinery corporations did the use of Gray's treadmills decline.

Then came another flood, which, although it did little serious damage, was to change the face, and even the name, of Middletown. After the waters receded, Albert Gray walked along the riverbanks to survey the damage and found that the old spring had been uncovered. With his sons, he began bottling and selling the springwater and launched plans for a grand spa hotel.

It was the era when taking the waters was not only thought to be healthy, but was highly fashionable as well. The Montvert Hotel, which opened in 1871, catered to its upper-crust clientele with every modern convenience. It was the biggest hotel in Vermont, four and a half stories high, with wide porches and large rooms, with gas lighting and a bell system in each room. It was the only hotel in Vermont that served dinner in the evening. (You will remember from Dorset that the early resorts here were farmhouses that took in guests and fed them farm-style, in the middle of the day.)

While the food was fresh from local farms, the chef and waiters were imported from New York, from the Hanover Hotel, where they "understand how dinner should be served," as the brochure promised. The hotel was set in parklike grounds along the riverbank, with a pathway leading from the front downhill and past flowerbeds to the springhouse. Every sort of curative spa treatment was offered, from "Turkish showers" to massages. They treated every ailment, from obesity to insomnia. The waters were considered highly effective for impotency, and the abundant size of local families was cited to prove the point. Evidently the New York clientele didn't consider the contributing factor of the long cold Vermont winters to this statistic.

Carriages met the trains in Poultney and Rutland. All this luxurious play involved the local people very little, except as a source of employment. The springs were indeed good for the health of the town, which changed its name in 1885 to Middletown Springs.

When the craze for springs began to decline, the modern Montvert was ready. Bicycles, riding stables, a bowling alley, a golf course, a croquet lawn, tennis courts, fishing, a full orchestra, and a whirl of social activities enabled the Montvert to make the transition to a resort hotel very smoothly. But it wasn't enough. Only the very wealthy could afford it, and they moved on to more fashionable venues. The hotel company went bankrupt in 1906, and the hotel was stripped and torn down. Its lumber was sold to build houses in nearby Poultney, and the bowling alley was torn down to build homes at the end of Montvert Avenue. These houses and the livery stable are still standing.

The floods of 1927, which destroyed so much all over Vermont, washed away the springhouse and again covered up the spring, but in 1970 it was uncovered again and a replica of the original springhouse was built from old illustrations, as a project of the overactive Middletown Springs Historical Society. The marble steps leading to the spring are original, found underneath the silt beside the river. The area is once again a park, with iron benches, picnic tables, and a signboard telling about the hotel and spring. The other small building in the park may have originally been the bottling plant for the springwater.

The Historical Society Building across the green displays the hotel china, menus, a wealth of old photographs, and other souvenirs of the Montvert. Also in its eclectic displays are treasures from the town's industrial, farming, and commercial past, including a fine example of one of Gray's horse-powered threshers. Because it was a stationary model, it was fixed permanently and spared the constant abuse of being hauled from farm to farm. Painted and decorated with freehand scrolls, striping, and stenciled eagles, the machine carries the logo: "The Best Horsepower in the U.S.—A. W. Gray's Sons."

The historical society sponsors a busy schedule of special events, including a summer picnic, a maple festival, and one of the finest Memorial Day parades of any small town. It's a real parade, with floats on tractors, kids on bikes, old carriages, and several bands.

The historical society was instrumental in getting the entire village center placed on the National Register of Historic Places, and it is always ready to provide expertise and help to anyone renovating or adding to a historic home or building. The town's architectural heritage is one of Middletown Springs's greatest treasures, so you can imagine the society's outrage when the Congregational Church, next door on the green, decided to build a modern addition directly adjoining the side of the historic church, instead of attaching it via a small connector, as the state Division for Historic Preservation had recommended, to maintain the integrity of the original church. One of the highlights of the historic green, the now-altered church is the second-oldest Congregational Church in the state, dating from 1796.

On the other side of the church is a fine example of a 19th-century Italianate home, with a metal filigree coaming on the roof, elaborate cornices, and a double-pillared porch. Inside, the detail is just as fine, with shoulder moldings surrounding doors and windows, stucco work, and faux burled panels in the doors. Built in the 1880s, the house never fell into disrepair; the woodwork has never been covered with paint nor the rooms remodeled, so it remains an almost perfect example of that style. Fortunately, it is open to the public as the Middletown Springs Inn, having previously been in the same family for about a century.

Across the green, at the corner of West and North Streets, is one of the most elaborate Federal-style homes in Middletown Springs. Built in 1814, it is the only brick house in the village, with parapet ends and marble trim. Right beside it on West Street is an outstanding 1840 Greek Revival home. At the corner of South Street and Burdock Avenue stands one of the oldest houses in the village, built in the 1790s. Continue down South Street past Montvert Avenue to see several other fine old homes of various styles, three of which belonged to the Gray family, whose several generations had brought prosperity, fame, and a change of name to Middletown Springs.

Places to See, Eat, and Stay

Middletown Springs Inn, On the Green, Box 1068, Middletown Springs 05757-1068; (802) 235-2198. The inn serves a fixed-menu dinner to overnight guests, by prior reservation, which is a good idea, since there is no other restaurant in town.

Strawberry Festival: for strawberry shortcake made with fresh-picked berries, visit Middletown Springs on the third Sunday in June. For details, call the Historical Society, (802) 235-2531.

Sugarhouse Gallery at Moonridge Farm, 350 Daisy Hollow Rd., Middletown Springs 05757; (802) 235-2434. Open Memorial Day weekend through foliage season, Monday through Tuesday and Thursday through Saturday, 10 A.M. to 5 P.M. Sugarhouse offers syrup, candy, and maple ice cream year-round; sugaring in the early spring; Morgan horses; and a crafts gallery.

Middletown Springs Historical Society, The Green, Middletown Springs 05757. The museum is open late June through foliage season, Sunday only, 2 P.M. to 4 P.M.

7

CHESTER:
VINTAGE
VICTORIAN

(CHESTER IS AT THE INTERSECTION OF ROUTES 11
AND 103, EIGHT MILES WEST OF SPRINGFIELD.)

If ever a town invited walking, it is Chester, whose well-kept homes and public buildings include 156 listed on the National Register of Historic Places, many of which stand within easy strolling distance of its green. An air of Victorian gentility prevails, and walking seems to be the proper pace at which to savor these extraordinary surroundings.

The buildings you will see on such a stroll are not just fine examples of their type. In many cases they are the finest examples. Nor do they stand, like peas in a pod, all of one style or era. They span the century from the 1820s to the 1920s, and show, in addition, how homes evolved in architecture to stay fashionable. You will see homes of the 1820s updated to the 1840s styles, and 1840s homes brought à la mode Victorian.

Chester was built in an era when its residents had the time for detail, and the decorations that embellished their homes were meant to be admired from the street. Begin at the little chamber of commerce kiosk, where Marie or another local resident will have plenty of time to share some anecdote of Chester's rich history and give you a copy of the walking-tour brochure. Its accurate and well-drawn illustrations (the work of Chester artist Lew Watters, who lives in the Stone Village) will help you identify the architectural styles, while Hugh Heary's equally good text will describe the 14 buildings on the tour in more detail than we do here.

This stroll around the green and along the radiating streets is a stroll through Chester's past and a good view of its present as well. As you go, you will meet local people and begin to notice that the separation between the town's past and its present is a very blurred line. But rather than living in their past, or worse yet, exploiting it to draw tourists, Chester people seem to involve their history into today's life just for fun—and often just for their own private pleasure.

The tiny Chamber kiosk sits almost directly on the sidewalk, facing the green. Behind it stands the commanding brick Academy building, built as the high school, replacing an older building erected when the private Chester Academy was founded in 1814. Educating both local and outside students, who boarded in local homes, the Academy was among the most respected in New England. It produced such a distinguished array of teachers, doctors, legislators, and public officials that it was once said that if the people of Chester had never done anything but maintain this Academy, "they would be entitled to the lasting gratitude of the world."

Replaced with a new high school, it is now home to the Chester Historical Society's collections and to the Chester Art Guild. In the summer, its ground floor shows works of local artists, and its upper floors are filled with historic collections. These include household furnishings of the 19th century, textiles and handwork, farm implements, and a collection of typewriters.

While the great variety of barns on Vermont's farms are among the state's "trademarks" to travelers, its village barns are no less interesting. Built for carriages and to house the teams that drew them, these carriage barns were not merely afterthoughts but were given serious architectural attention. The small carriage barn next to the Academy, at the Hugging Bear shop, is a fine, although fairly small, example of this type of architecture at the turn of the 20th century, with a gable and cupola. The shop itself is filled with bears of every variety, stacked in a profusion of furriness from floor to ceiling.

This entire side of the street is lined with houses that invite a closer look, including the distinguished Chester House, with its series of attached outbuildings, and the Queen Anne next to it, with the corner tower distinctive of that style. At the corner of Main and Church Streets stands one of Vermont's finest examples of a Federal-style church. Its pedimented entrance draws the eye upward to a "five-layer" bell and clock tower reminiscent of Bulfinch's work. The church was built in 1828 with the cooperation of three different denominations, each of which took its turn holding services there. It became the Congregational Church in the 1840s.

Next to the church is a house that was originally built in the simpler classical Greek Revival style, about 1840. But to keep up with the fashions of the later part of the Victorian era, it was dressed up with the addition of a variety of fancy decorations. The three little finials on the pediment over the front door are very typical of the Gothic Revival. Beyond are two stone houses, of which you will see an outstanding collection in the northern village along Route 103.

The two brick houses and the clapboard house opposite the intersection of Main Street and Lovers Lane are all Federal style, part of the early settlement of Chester's Main Street and built about 1820.

Returning along the south side of Main Street, you will come to the Inn Victoria, in yet another architectural style and the only French Second Empire house in Chester. Popular for its afternoon teas, this inn is decorated in period antiques, with luxuries the Victorian traveler never dreamed of. The little building next door, once the office of the doctor who owned the house, is now the Tea Pot Shoppe, with fine teas and accessories.

Next door is St. Luke's Episcopal Church, a Gothic Revival classic. It has all the hallmarks of its style, including the little buttresses, the pointed arch windows, and the spire rising from square to octagonal. The only variation is the clapboard siding instead of the more commonly seen board-and-batten. Inside, the church is pristine, with carved oak woodwork and stained glass.

Directly on the green, The Chester Inn at Long Last, built in 1921, was the fifth inn to occupy that position. Beyond the inn is Misty Valley Books, with a good selection of reading matter on Vermont.

A turn down School Street, which you can cross at the corner of Canal Street, brings you to the Rose Arbour, an inviting B&B with a tearoom. Kathy, who does the cooking, moved to town shortly after her parents bought the fine old Victorian home, and she soon married the local Baptist minister, a happy-ending story the locals love to tell about. She has worked for so long to perfect her tea scones that when the magazine *Victoria* asked for the recipe, she turned them down politely, despite the publicity it would have brought her newly opened tearoom. These scones are well worth traveling for. A shop filled with tasteful Victorian and other items adjoins in the parlor.

Back on Main Street just around the corner is one of the finest examples of Queen Anne residences in the state. No detail was spared in applying ornament to this 1900 house.

No matter how many times you pass this building, you never fail to notice some feature you've missed before. Even in a town so rich in fine Victorian homes, this one is a showstopper.

Next door is the Whiting Library, completed in 1892 on the design of a Vermont architect. It combines art nouveau with Queen Anne styles, with a horseshoe-shaped window and marble arches framing all the windows. The interior is in oak paneling.

The Baptist Church, back at the head of the green, is unusual for its slate-covered tower, which was once the base for a tall spire, also in slate. The spire was removed in 1940. Between the church and the Academy, and stretching back into the fields behind the Main Street houses, is the town's walled cemetery. Its stone vault, with the date carved prominently above the door, served more than the usual purpose. In the winter, when the ground was frozen, vaults were used as storage facilities. But in the early (and even later) 19th century, grave robbing was a serious problem. There was almost no legal way for medical schools to obtain bodies in order to teach anatomy or for surgical practice. The body of an occasional criminal was turned over to them, but that was far from enough. So they hired agents to "resurrect" freshly buried ones.

These specialists were quite good at it, and could usually rob a grave so neatly and quickly that the family was none the wiser. To prevent this, sextons would keep bodies in the vaults, where they could be locked securely, until they were no longer useful to medical schools, before burying them. While it thwarted the thieves, it certainly didn't make the job of sexton a popular one.

In July, Chester's centrally located cemetery is the scene of ghostly doings during the Victorian Ghosts and Gossamer

Weekend. The lawn of the Academy next door is transformed into a canopied dance floor for the gala costume ball that highlights the weekend, and dancers are treated to occasional glimpses of the mysterious woman in blue of local folklore.

The story—highly embellished, we suspect—is that a young woman fell in love with a local carpenter who was doing some work for her father. Papa forbade them to see each other and kept a very close watch on her. The carpenter later married someone else. After her father died, the heartbroken girl, who always wore pale blue, frequently strolled past the home of her former lover, who grew more and more reclusive. One day, she rode out of town past his home in her carriage, and within an hour her fine home burned to the ground. While she was never heard of again, locals later reported seeing her near his home. When he died, not long afterward, a small bouquet of blue gentians, without a card, appeared at his graveside.

This mysterious lady in blue has become the theme of this annual weekend, attended by both locals and visitors, most of whom dress in turn-of-the-century costumes. Local inns serve tea and put croquet sets on their lawns. Other genteel games, period crafts, historic walking tours, an Edwardian fashion show, a "town ball" game (early baseball), and dramatic and musical events fill two days with gaiety and the town with colorful costumes that look right at home against the backdrop of Victorian architecture.

Early in its history, the town was divided into two parishes, with the Baptists settling at the site of the present Baptist Church, and the Congregationalists settling along the stagecoach route north of town, on what is now Route 103. When the railroad line opened in 1849, it passed between them, not terribly convenient to either, but a fairly divided distance. A third village, the Depot, sprung up near the tracks. Today, the South Parish is the center of Chester, almost melded into the settlement at the Depot, while the North Parish remains spread in two tidy lines along the highway.

The railway station, a classic restored to its original appearance, is once again an active terminal, at least during the summer and fall. The Green Mountain Flyer, a sightseeing train, operates on the 26 miles of track between Chester and Bellows Falls. For a minimal extra fare, you can ride in one of the two fully restored classic wooden coaches, either the 1913 or the 1891 car, possibly the oldest passenger car still in regular revenue service in New England. On the way, the train passes two covered bridges and pauses for a heart-stopping few minutes on the trestle astride the plunging walls of Brockaway Gorge.

Near the depot is the impressive town hall, built in 1884, and a short distance beyond it stands the unusual Yosemite Fire Company building, a former firehouse with a tall tower used to dry hoses after use. Inside is a collection of early equipment used in firefighting; the building and collections are the property of the Chester Historical Society.

At the corner where the road crosses a brook and is joined by the Old Green Mountain Turnpike, an old mill sits overlooking the water. It was the scene, in 1902, of the climax of one of Chester's—and Vermont's—most bizarre criminal cases. But our story begins some years earlier.

In September 1886, a burglar (or burglars) broke into Chester's Adams and David Company, removing money from the safe. It was a well-done job, and the culprit was never caught. Within the next 16 years, over 50 robberies in town joined this one in the files of unsolved cases. There was increasing evidence to suggest that the crimes were committed by the same person (and sometimes persons). For one thing, they were all very cleverly arranged, often taking more trouble than was necessary by entering in some ingenious way. The thief seemed to enjoy the challenge as much as the loot.

Some stores were robbed more than once, and unusual things were taken: a new bicycle, ladies' gloves, shingles, and with a frequency that alarmed the mill owner, bags of feed from the mill. On the rare occasion when there was a witness, no identification was ever made. Most of the thefts involved stores, but a few were in private homes. No one seemed safe, and the store owners became nearly desperate. Burglar alarms did no good; in fact, they seemed to attract the criminal, who clearly enjoyed finding the one spot they didn't cover.

After repeated appeals from merchants and others, the selectmen offered a five-hundred-dollar reward for the capture of the thief. Although that was a substantial incentive in itself, the embarrassed first selectman, Clarence Adams, upped the ante with one hundred dollars from his own pocket. But when a local merchant stocked revolvers for the townspeople to protect themselves, they were stolen from his store.

After Charles Waterman, owner of the mill over the brook, had been hit several times, he began to notice a pattern to the crimes. The thief's signature seemed to be that he entered through the most unlikely means, and Waterman acted on the hunch that the thief would eventually try to get in through the window above the raceway to the mill. Requiring no little skill, and nerves of steel, entrance could be gained from the roof of a small ell nearby. With luck it would not include a fall into the water.

Waterman rigged a shotgun to fire directly at anyone who managed to raise the sash. He told no one, not even his friend, the first selectman, who had helped him try to protect his property in the past. When the shotgun went off in the night, the thief escaped, but the blood on the windowsill told Waterman he'd hit his man.

That same night, Selectman Adams, the same one who had offered the additional reward, was shot and robbed in his wagon as he went home to his farm. While the town buzzed with outrage—Adams was a very popular man, a library trustee, and representative to the legislature—the constable doggedly began his investigation of both crime sites. He found, to his surprise, no blood on the wagon seat where Adams claimed to have been sitting at the time of the attack, only in the back, where he was found. And there were no footprints in the dirt at the alleged scene of the shooting. Furthermore, the buckshot removed from Adams's leg matched that of the rigged booby trap.

A search of the Adams farm turned up much of the property that had been stolen over the years, an odd assortment stored in the barn. Although no one in Chester could believe it, the evidence was almost indisputable, and Adams pleaded guilty when charged.

He was sentenced to 10 years in the Windsor prison, where he was a model prisoner. Two years later he died. But the story didn't end there. A month or so later, someone saw Adams in Canada, and even spoke with him enough to be sure it was the same man. When news of this reached home, it triggered an investigation of the circumstances surrounding his death. A number of questions were raised. First, how did a perfectly healthy man come to die after only two days' illness? Why did the doctor sign the death certificate without examination, simply on the assurance of an orderly—an inmate himself and close friend of Adams? And why was the body left unattended in the prison and later in the back room of the undertaker's store? Did anyone who knew Adams, except for the fellow prisoner and his closest friend, ever see the body? Exhumation proved inconclusive, since some time had elapsed, and no one ever knew for sure whether the Chester burglar made it to the grave or safely to Canada.

Waterman's Mill is now the Grist Mill Gallery, showing paintings and other works. They'll point out the window to you, and even sell you an excellent little booklet reprinting an article from *Vermont Life* that describes the event in full detail. The original window sash is at the historical society.

The South Parish grew and prospered. By 1830, there were nine sawmills, five stores, six taverns, four tanneries, a distillery, and several other mills when the two Clark brothers, who had learned stonemasonry in Canada, began to build homes along North Street using stone quarried from the hill to the east. The result is one of the finest stone villages still in existence. A school, a church, and close to 30 gray stone houses still stand in two neat rows facing each other across Route 103.

When one of these was being remodeled, a small room with an exit to the carriage shed was found hidden beneath the kitchen. Since Chester is known to have been a way station on the Underground Railroad, it is very likely that this was one of the houses used by escaped slaves.

Hospitality has been a strong tradition in Chester from its earliest days. Its position at the crossing of two well-traveled routes—one of them among the few across the Green Mountains—as well as the railroad, made it a stopping point for travelers. In addition, students at the Academy boarded in local homes. The tradition remains, with an abundance of interesting lodgings, most of them historic. Along with those already mentioned in the stroll around the village, several lie in the quiet of the surrounding hills.

The most historic of these is Rowell's Inn, an 1820 stagecoach stop west of the village. It was renovated (still as an inn) in 1900, when its fine tin ceilings, central heating, and other "modern" improvements were added. Today it offers rooms furnished in period pieces, as well as fine dining with a fixed menu for inn guests only. Its three-story porches make this landmark easy to spot.

Rowell's Inn

Not so easy to find, but well worth the search, is The Inn at High View, reached through the tiny village of Andover. The gardens are at their height in June, but all summer their colorful blossoms provide the foreground for the sweeping mountain views only available from such a hilltop setting.

Overlooking the Williams River, close to Brockaway Gorge, is the newly built Madrigal Inn. Its soaring living room with a balcony was designed for chamber music, and in December it hosts a concert series. If you have any interest in how a fine building is constructed and maintained, ask for a full tour while you are staying there. The system that ensures a constant supply of hot water for guests is amazing. The Chester area, with its appreciation for architectural niceties, is a highly appropriate setting for a place of Madrigal's integrity.

Places to See, Eat, and Stay

Rowell's Inn, RR 1, Box 269, Chester 05143; (802) 875-3658. Rooms on the third floor each reward those who don't mind steep steps with half a ballroom, complete with rounded ceilings and elegant furnishings.

The Inn at High View, RR 1, Box 201A, Andover 05143; (802) 875-2724. On weekends, opt for the Italian dinner, served only to overnight guests.

The Rose Arbour Tea Room, Gift Shop and B&B, School St., Chester 05143; (802) 875-4767. Open Tuesday through Saturday 10 A.M. to 5 P.M., Sunday noon to 5 P.M.

Madrigal Inn, 61 Williams River Rd., Chester 05143; (802) 463-1339 or (800) 854-2208.

Inn Victoria, On the Green, Chester 05143; (802) 875-4288 or (800) 732-4288.

The Green Mountain Flyer, P.O. Box 498, Bellows Falls 05101; (802) 463-3069. The train operates late June through early September, and during the height of foliage season, daily except Monday. Early and late in the season it runs weekend days only, so it's important to call for exact dates and to make reservations.

Chester Historical Society and Chester Art Guild, On the Green, Chester 05143; (802) 875-3767. Open June through October, Tuesday through Sunday 2 to 5 P.M.

8

ISLAND POND: CAPITAL OF THE NORTHEAST KINGDOM WILDERNESS

(ISLAND POND IS AT THE JUNCTION OF ROUTES 105 AND 114, 32 MILES NORTH OF ST. JOHNSBURY.)

Moose, spruce, and some of the wildest land in Vermont surround Island Pond. While the Northeast Kingdom includes most of Orleans, Caledonia, and Essex counties, the only really large wild areas are the two huge tracts northeast and southeast of Island Pond, separated only by the solitary Route 105, which leads to the New Hampshire border. Covering the region is a boreal forest, a type of woodland that grows in the coldest places on earth and that stretches to the Arctic. Within this area of approximately 750 square miles there is no settlement, but abundant wildlife of all kinds. During a visit to the area in 1949 Putney Senator George Aiken remarked to a group of people in Lyndonville that "this is such a beautiful country up here. It ought to be called the Northeast Kingdom of Vermont." His vision has become a title the area carries proudly.

The first time history mentions this area is during the French and Indian Wars, when Rogers's Rangers raided the French and Indian settlement at Saint Francis, on the Saint Francis River north of Lake Champlain. Kenneth Roberts immortalized the assault in his novel *Northwest Passage*. On the night of October 4, 1759, the Rangers attacked the settlement from which almost all of the vicious raids against English settlements had been launched. When they began their raid they found the scalps of six hundred English settlers waving from poles in the encampment.

While they were able to totally destroy the village, the Rangers were immediately pursued by French and Indian forces. Plunging into the wilderness with gold coin, silver plates, and an eight-pound silver image of the Virgin from the plundered town and chapel, Rogers's forces split up into several smaller groups at Barton, and one of these groups, believed to be the one carrying the silver image, went east to the Nulhegan River at present-day Island Pond. They followed the river to the Connecticut River, but promised support was not there. Alone and starving, they allowed an Indian to lead them toward Mount Washington, stopping to bury their treasure. Almost all of the men perished along the way. Periodically, as settlers came into the area they found bones and rusted guns. Part of the gold coin and a pair of gold candlesticks were found, but the silver image of the Virgin still lies buried somewhere in the forest.

It wasn't until the heyday of the railroads in the middle of the 19th century that any serious attention was paid to the area at the head of Island Pond. Canadians were looking for a rail route to a port that didn't freeze over in the winter, and New Englanders wanted a way to tap the resources, particularly timber, of the northern parts of New Hampshire and Vermont. In 1845 the Atlantic and St. Lawrence Railroad was chartered in Maine and two years later in New Hampshire. By 1853 it reached all the way to North Stratford, New Hampshire, and the Canadians had completed their Canadian National Railroad to the Canadian border.

The pioneering railroad planner John A. Poor dreamed of an international railroad linking Montreal with Portland, Maine, and in 1853 the Grand Trunk Railroad started the final linking of the two lines. On July 18, 1854, the first international railroad on the North American continent was completed.

The American and Canadian lines met at the head of Island Pond, a large lake with a 22-acre island in it. The settlement that grew there was called Random, but it quickly adopted the name of the pond. Island Pond became a village in the town of Brighton. The railroad was the reason for the town and dominated the place from the very beginning. At its height, 13 sets of tracks passed through the middle of town, and the railyard was so busy that a wooden bridge had to be built over the tracks to connect the residential section on the adjoining hill with the business district at the head of the lake.

With a ready means to transport freight, the timber on the surrounding hills assumed new importance. As early as 1864, many of the neighboring hillsides were cleared and the head of the lake was filled with floating logs awaiting processing and transport to market. Only 10 years after the linking of the railroads, Island Pond was a sizable community of two-story frame houses and manufacturing plants along the lakefront. Business blocks rose along the streets, and the enormous brick and granite two-story railroad station announced that this was an important town that was here to stay. Spared from a massive forest fire that destroyed much of the surrounding land in 1855, a new residential section of fine Victorian houses on the eastern hillside overlooked the busy town below.

The prosperity continued for almost three quarters of a century until the Depression in the 1930s, when the town's industry began a slow and painful decline; the railroad fell into disuse after World War II. Of the once-numerous furniture plants, the most significant remaining one is the Ethan Allen Furniture Company, two miles east of town on Route 105.

If Island Pond were a corporation, it would describe itself as downsizing and reshaping itself to a new role as a center for outdoor recreation and sports. Many of the two- and three-story business blocks are now gone. The development of its downtown never reached the point of fancy buildings, and the pleasant, utilitarian blocks that remain give it the air of a frontier town, even today.

The impression carries even to the hill above the railway station, where there are some fine examples of late Victorian buildings, such as the classic board-and-batten Gothic Christ Episcopal Church and the Saint James Catholic Church, which has a very attractive but unusual steeple.

Religion propelled Island Pond into the national headlines in June of 1984, when reports of severe child abuse led Vermont authorities to raid the homes of members of a religious community and seize 112 children in an effort to determine if there had been physical abuse. In the 1970s members of a Tennessee religious group had moved to Island Pond and established the Northeast Kingdom Community Church. Based on very fundamental principles, the community held among its tenets a belief in the physical disciplining of children. During the course of divorce proceedings between couples, in which one partner had left the Community and the other remained, allegations of systematic and prolonged child beating had arisen. While Community members had lived in the town in peace with their neighbors for a long time, the allegations and the raid that followed raised the specter of cult excesses and severely disrupted community relationships. After the raid, a hearing in a Vermont State District Court resulted in a dismissal of the complaint, and the children were returned to their homes.

After the raid the Community stayed in town and continued to operate their businesses. Slowly the strained relationships mended, and the doubts of both sides have begun to soften. In 1994, on the 10th anniversary of the raid, the Community held a commemoration at another of its settlements in Westminster, Vermont. Most of the participants in the raid, from all sides, were invited, and several of the children, now adults, spoke about their experiences of and reactions to the raid.

The feeling of the town is probably best summed up by the comments of a man in Island Pond who told us, "While I really don't take to their religion, I've got to say that I've watched them with their kids, and you'll see them walking down the street, hand in hand and all smiles. Those kids are obviously important to them and they love them." Like the people of Putney, whom you'll meet later, Island Pond residents have a live-and-let-live philosophy and a healthy respect for the right to live according to one's own beliefs.

On Cross Street, overlooking the lake, is the Lakefront Motel, which has come to be a center for the "repositioning" of Island Pond as a sports center. The two-story motel has bright, clean, and nicely decorated rooms and efficiency units as well as two large suites. Harry Burnham, an avid rower, put Island Pond on the sports map with his sculling programs and canoe rentals run from the hotel, and although Harry no longer does the sculling weekends, the motel has continued the canoe rentals. Their new docks are available to guests who have their own boats, and the motel rents a sailboat and a fishing boat.

During the summer, Maurice Barnes operates scenic narrated lake tours on his *Lady of the Lake*, a stable and smooth-riding pontoon boat. During the hour-long tour of Island Pond, you can eat your picnic lunch and bask in the sun and fresh air while the points of interest are described. The boat has pickup spots at Lakeside Camping, the Senior Center, and the Lakefront Motel dock.

On the thin spit of land that separates Island Pond from Spectacle Pond, Brighton State Park offers camping and opportunities for boating on both ponds. Spectacle Pond is an unusual geological feature known as a kettle. It was formed when a large piece of the last glacier broke off and became embedded in the debris sloughed off by the retreating glacier. After the glacier melted away, the buried piece slowly melted and the thin layer of debris over it collapsed into the space. Barely 10 feet at its deepest, the pond and the area around it offer a microcosm of the plant and animal life of a northern pond and shore. It is a popular place with native animals; deer, moose, black bear, bobcat, raccoon, and squirrels have all been seen along its shores. Spectacle Pond even has a nesting pair of loons, which should not be approached. A half-mile marked nature trail along the shore can be combined with another trail to make a one-mile walk.

In the winter Island Pond becomes a mecca for snowmobilers, who come from all over the northeast. While the frozen surfaces of the many area lakes provide outstanding riding, there are also miles of trails through the neighboring forests and into Canada, a short distance away. The lakefront is the center for this sport, too, with new garage facilities and a full-service sales and rental dealer directly across the street. Snowmobile tours can be arranged from there as well.

Diagonally across the street from the lakefront is the Clyde River Coffee Shop, in a renovated older business block. The food is good and plentiful, and the prices are low. The breakfast menu, available all day, offers thermos fills of coffee for $1.25; daily lunch specials are in the five-dollar range. The coffee shop is in the Clyde River Hotel, which offers inexpensive rooms, some with kitchenettes, and special weekend and weekly rates.

Jennifer's, on the other end of Cross Street, serves breakfast, lunch, and dinner in portions "you can barely hope to plow a path through," as one local resident describes them. It's no wonder it is busy at peak eating hours. We should also mention the Buck 'n' Doe, opposite the railway station. Whenever Island Pond comes into the conversation, someone will mention this restaurant. Unfortunately, it has closed, but it will take a long time for the memory to die.

The wilderness surrounding Island Pond, and the nature of the terrain, make it an outstanding setting for biking, mountain biking, hiking, and walking—and for cross-country skiing and snowshoeing in the winter. Most of the land surrounding the town is owned by lumber companies, and the forests are laced with logging roads that reach deep into the woods. You could hike practically every day and not do the same path twice in a year.

The woods, fields, and mountains are also well known for some of the best birding in the state. Harry Burnham reports having seen, among others, the gray jay and Blackburnian warbler, and while walking in the Moose Bog in Winlock Wildlife Preserve he encountered a spruce grouse in the path.

As Island Pond repositions itself for the growing interest in outdoor and nature-based recreation, its residents needn't worry about being overrun by tourists; the wilderness that surrounds them has plenty of space left.

Places to See, Eat, and Stay

Lakefront Motel, Cross St., Box 161, Island Pond 05846; (802) 723-6507. Single rooms, efficiencies, and suites; a new carriage shed is available for snowmobile maintenance, and new docks provide facilities for boats.

Clyde River Hotel, c/o Bernard Wilson, Cross St., Island Pond 05846; (802) 723-4458. Some of the rooms are kitchenette-equipped, all are inexpensive.

Jeannine's B&B, Jeannine Clarke, Middle St., P.O. Box 245, Island Pond 05846; (802) 723-6673. B&B serving continental breakfast.

Clyde River Coffee Shop, Cross St., Island Pond 05846; (802) 723-4540. Open until 3 P.M. for breakfast and lunch only.

Jennifer's Restaurant, Cross St., Island Pond 05846; (802) 723-6135. Serving inexpensive and hearty breakfast, lunch, and dinner.

Barnes Recreation, Maurice Barnes, RR 1, Box 194, Island Pond 05846; (802) 723-6649. Boat rides on Island Pond.

Bob Halpin, Island Pond 05846; (802) 723-9702. Snowmobile rentals.

Brighton State Park, Off of Route 5, Island Pond 05846; (802) 723-4360 (summer); (802) 479-4280 (winter). Open mid-May through Columbus Day for camping, hiking, nature walks, swimming.

9
WAITSFIELD:
THE FINE BALANCE
OF FARMING
AND SKIING

(WAITSFIELD IS ON ROUTE 100,
19 MILES SOUTHWEST OF MONTPELIER.)

The town of Waitsfield was not chartered by Royal Governors of New Hampshire or New York, nor by the state of Vermont. When General Benjamin Wait applied for a charter in 1782, it was to the independent Republic of Vermont, not yet admitted to the new United States.

The general had made his name—and rank—through long military service that began at the age of 18 in the French and Indian Wars. He was a member of the Green Mountain Boys and had distinguished himself as a captain, then a colonel, under George Washington. When he came to settle the grant in 1789, he brought with him 13 others, 11 of whom were also veterans of the Revolution. Tradition holds that of the group, six had served with the Minutemen at Lexington and Concord.

Wait himself had lived for some time in the town of Windsor, where he had been a community leader, high sheriff, and representative to Vermont's Constitutional Conventions. At 53, he moved his family to the unsettled land of the Mad River Valley and again became a pillar of his community. He was active as selectman, representative to the legislature, and leader of his church, until he died at age 86.

His home served for some years as the center of village life—town meetings were in his parlor, church services in his barn. Such early commerce and industry as there was took place on the high ground above the river, not on the floor of the valley where the town later grew. A store, a cabinetmaker, a tannery, a blacksmith shop, and a meetinghouse served the community, which had grown to 50 families by the turn of the century.

From the first, residents had an eye toward improving their town. They voted a tax of two pence an acre, half of which was to be spent on roads and bridges and the other half to attract new industry and commerce. This forerunner to the chamber of commerce offered a tax subsidy, and soon there were gristmills and sawmills along the river south of the village, in the settlement called Iraville today. It was named for an early resident, Ira Richardson, not for Ethan's brother Ira Allen, as sometimes suggested.

New roads were laid out and bridges built, including the covered bridge over the Mad River at what was known as the Great Eddy. The bridge still stands, the second oldest in the state and the oldest in steady use. Slowly, the commercial center of the village shifted to the area around the bridge and onto the new road, called the Mad River Turnpike, which is Route 100 today. A hotel was built on the corner, and the series of porticoed stores that still stand today. A complex of gristmills and sawmills rose on the east side of the covered bridge, and a canal was dug to provide them with power.

It was during the first third of the 19th century that most of the buildings that now give the village of Waitsfield its charm and character were constructed. Over 70 of these are listed as historic buildings in the Waitsfield Historic District, notable as almost entirely intact from that period.

Farming was the basis for the community, with lumber, potash, and maple sugar supplementing cash crops of grain and potatoes. Like a number of other towns, Waitsfield offered a deduction from property taxes based on the number of sheep sheared. By 1826 the Grand List (property inventory) for the town showed 3,212 sheep and only 550 head of cattle.

Like most farming towns of its day, Waitsfield was fairly self-sufficient, growing, processing, and manufacturing most of its necessities, supporting its citizens in times of need, and providing whatever social, cultural, and spiritual activity as there was time for. Eighty percent of the town's families engaged in farming. Even men who worked in the mills or operated businesses often kept farm animals to provide meat, eggs, and dairy products. A horse was almost a necessity for transportation.

The situation remained much the same for the next century, with families producing most of what they ate and selling the extras or trading them for needed commodities. Sheep were replaced by dairy herds, as was happening throughout the state of Vermont in the middle of the century. Milk and cream were made into cheese and butter and shipped to markets throughout New England. By 1880 Waitsfield had 135 farms, and its land, except for the highest and steepest mountain slopes, was largely cleared.

The towns around Waitsfield—Moretown, Warren, and Fayston—provided markets for agricultural goods, too. Moretown and Warren were lumbering and mill centers, rough-and-tumble places, with less farming than Waitsfield. Fayston had farms, but it was also primarily a lumber town, and had no real village center. Built on hillsides overlooking the valley, its natural lines of communication ran downhill into Waitsfield, and it was hard to construct roads across the mountain shoulders. So the natural direction for Fayston residents to go for their commerce was Waitsfield, which soon became the commercial center for all four towns.

Life was difficult on those early farms, most of them remote from the village center and even from each other. Roads were poor, and for more than half the year they were snow-covered or deep in mud. Sleds were used as much as wagons, and in the winter instead of plowing snow away, they rolled it with a huge drum to create a hard-packed surface. By spring, the many layers of packed snow made the roadways several feet higher than the surrounding fields. As this mound began to melt away, it was almost impossible to drive a horse or team over it.

Until the 1830s, valley families used two-wheeled carts. The first four-wheeled cart owned in the valley came by barge in the 1830s as far as Burlington and then was shipped to Starksboro, which is on the other side of the Green Mountains, opposite Waitsfield. (At this time, there was no road connecting the valley to the towns north of it in the Winooski Valley.) Each day, the farmer left home and went over the mountain, returning with as much of the wagon as he could carry—a wheel, pieces of frame, axles—until, after 10 days, he had all the parts and could assemble his wagon to haul lumber.

Social life called for the same resourcefulness and was often combined with work, especially when a job required more hands than a single farm could muster. Barn raisings, where a number of families pitched in, were a welcome change from the everyday routine, and a social occasion as well as a working one.

One particular type of social event recalled by older valley residents continued well into the 20th century. They were called, curiously, "kitchen junkets," and they always included dancing. Good dance callers might sing or call the dance steps, accompanied by a fiddle or several instruments. During the evening, there would be several breaks when everyone ate. These kitchen junkets were a particular specialty of neighboring Warren, and many proper Waitsfield girls weren't allowed to go to them.

The traditions of Waitsfield's farming history are still strong, and they provide some of the favorite activities for visitors and local residents even today. Sleigh rides, once a necessity, are now recreation; Lareau Farm Country Inn offers sleigh rides in their meadow, along the edge of the woods, and beside the river. On Halloween, Hartshorn's Farmstand has a display of about a thousand carved pumpkins, and local farmers bring their fresh flowers and produce to a farmer's market every Saturday during the season. Herbs are Nancy Scarzello's passion, and she shares her plants and products at Maple Spring Farm. Her display gardens are open to the public, and Nancy teaches about herbs at her workshops and on her seasonal wild herb walks. A small shop sells tea and culinary blends along with other herbal products.

Maple sugar and syrup, once produced on almost every farm in the area, are still the primary business of Everett and Catherine Palmer. Everett was one of the first to realize that his sugaring business had to take advantage of modern technology if it were to survive. Plastic tubing has replaced buckets, and about half the water is extracted from sap by a reverse osmosis system. Palmer Sugar House was built in 1840, and still looks pretty much as it did then. Catherine serves doughnuts and sour pickles to accompany the traditional maple sugar on snow, a treat available during the sugaring season in late February and early March. Palmer syrup continues to take awards and blue ribbons, just as it did in the days when school closed for sugaring season so everyone could help haul sap from the woods.

A landmark of the valley's agricultural past is the great round Joslyn Barn on East Warren Road. Round barns, while never plentiful in Vermont (where only 24 are known to have been built), were not an uncommon sight in the valley of the Mad River, where they stood on four different farms.

Originated by the Shakers, round barns had a number of advantages over the traditional rectangular barn. For one thing, the farmer didn't have to back a vehicle in or out. He could drive a team or a truck in, load or unload, and drive right around and out. The raceway provided an entrance directly into the top for hay storage, and the middle level housed the dairy cows, which were also easier to herd in and out in a circle. Beneath the stanchions, trap doors allowed the manure to be shoveled directly into trucks waiting below on the ground level.

The Joslyn Round Barn was built in 1910 by Clem Joslyn and, like the farm, stayed in the family and was used as a dairy barn until 1969. Marge Joslyn, wife of the last generation's owner, is reputed to have told her husband, "Either the cows go or I go," and he gave up dairy farming.

The Simkos, who had been in the flower business for many years, bought the property in 1986 and, after restoring the farmhouse and converting it to a luxurious and comfortable inn, set about restoring the barn. It took them two years. They began by jacking up the entire structure and pouring a new foundation to replace the crumbling stone one. They replaced the cedar shakes and reroofed it, adding insulation. Rotting timbers were replaced, but essentially the barn was solid.

"I like the idea of people buying old farms and fixing them up, instead of building new," Doreen Simko says of their long years of work. But then they had to decide exactly what they would do with it.

"Here we were with this barn, which cost a fortune to restore, which was costing us more money in taxes, the uses of which were limited by zoning restrictions. We wanted the community to have access to it. We thought of studios for artists and craftsmen, but zoning prohibited any retail sales in it. We knew craftspeople needed to be able to sell their work. Then a couple asked to be married at the inn, and we realized what a real potential we had there for weddings."

Doreen wanted more than that, however, and envisioned the barn as a home for cultural events. "I wanted the Vermont Symphony playing, with Leonard Bernstein conducting. We got the symphony, but not Bernstein," she laughs. Friends helped, and the Simkos paid for the event out of ticket sales. That's when the idea of the Green Mountain Cultural Center was born.

The center now has more than two hundred members and presents performing and visual arts as well as hands-on workshops throughout the year. The Vermont Mozart Festival, pianists, brass ensembles, Elizabeth von Trapp, and an annual art show fill a busy schedule. At Christmas the whole town joins in the Fantasy of Christmas Trees and a community sing. These events do not bring business to the inn, Doreen observes, but they bring cultural events to the valley for everyone to enjoy, and they bring life back to the old barn and make it available for everyone to see and enjoy.

On Sunday mornings, the ground floor is transformed into St. Dunstan's Episcopal Church, with parishioners literally setting up and striking the chairs, organ, altar, and pulpit each week. This unusual parish arrangement is the work of the 50 or so regular members from the valley, working

Round Barn Farm

together, as one of them expressed it, "in exactly the same way farm families have always made this valley a community." The priest-in-charge is a member of the congregation, who is quick to point out that the members themselves are the real ministers, handling the work of pastoral calls and parish administration. As parishioner Mary Kerr puts it, "Without clapboard, bricks, or mortar of its own, St. Dunstan's continues to flourish." And so does the historic round barn.

The story of the barn is illustrative of the plight of farms throughout the valley. Faced with one of the highest tax rates in the state, depressed prices on agricultural products, the competition from larger mechanized farms elsewhere, and the pressure of the real estate market to build summer homes on the high pasture lands, farmers are caught in the crunch.

Waitsfield's population is now weighted in favor of newcomers, who expect the community services they had in the urban areas they left. They are more used to paying for these services than providing them through community effort, and so the tax burden increases. That hits the farmers, who own the most land, the hardest. Everyone agrees on the importance of keeping the land open, but the pressure falls on the farmer who owns it.

While the opening of the Sugarbush ski area in 1958 gave the area a much-needed shot in the arm, it caused problems, too. As the facilities of the ski area expanded at the mountain, skiers didn't need to come down to the village for lodging and meals. But the increasing number of seasonal homes being built created pressures for the year-round community. Sugarbush became the darling of the jet set (some say the term was coined here) and the division grew between the quiet Vermont town and the international clientele après-skiing at Club 10. But places are only fashionable for so long, and the winter jet set moved on to whiter pastures, leaving an infrastructure that keeps Sugarbush high on the list of the finest places to ski in the east.

The local community is far more involved now, as many skiers prefer to stay in traditional older inns. In addition, skiers who first see the area in the winter return to enjoy it in other seasons. Mascara Mountain no more, Sugarbush has grown to be a part of the valley it overlooks, both as an employer and a consumer of local services. But the integration has not been without casualties.

Vacation homes, locals feel, started the whole cycle for the farmer. In order to remain profitable, a farm needs to have a minimum of 80 in its dairy herd. That assumes that the wife works full time and has a benefit package to cover health insurance. In order to raise the feed necessary for the herd, most farmers lease adjacent land. When they put their own land into conservation easements in order to lower its tax rate, they make that decision based on the availability of neighboring land for grain production.

But when the real estate pressures for vacation homes woo that neighboring land, and it is sold for house lots, the farmer can no longer raise enough grain to feed the herd. And so he is left with the choice of cutting his herd to an unprofitable level or selling his own land. And yet, somehow, the farms do survive. Young farmers like David DeFreest, who has increased the herd on his family farm to eight hundred, work hours a corporate executive would never tolerate, then stay up the rest of the night trying to figure out where to grow a few more acres of corn. And because of them, Waitsfield still retains its rural character of unbroken meadows and hill farms.

"These are real people living here," DeFreest's mother-in-law over at the Inn at the Round Barn, adds. "We want it to look nice for the people who come here, but people live here, too. We can't just laminate it."

For all the Natural Historic Register quality of its village and the open landscapes of its farms, Waitsfield doesn't seem in danger of lamination. But it does have a few of its own idiosyncrasies that make newcomers stop short in disbelief. For example, when they first try to make a call from a public telephone, they discover that there's no place to put the coins. They can just dial their local number and the phone rings. Free public phones are just one of the advantages to having a private telephone company.

In the late 19th century, after Bell Telephone had begun connecting the nation via the telephone wire, it was difficult for small communities to get a phone system. Urban areas offered more profit for less line. Rural areas were left to fend for themselves, which they did with the help of some handy how-to booklets from Montgomery Ward. It was not at all uncommon for outlying farms to string up wires along the fenceposts to connect to friends and family several miles away. Sometimes several of these lines were combined and connected into an exchange that allowed contact with the outside world.

In 1904, a group of local residents petitioned for the incorporation of the Waitsfield and Fayston Telephone Company, which was similar to other local companies across the country. The switchboard was in a private home, and all calls had to be connected by hand. Some lines had as many as 15 families on a "party line"—imagine the opportunities for listening in—so a five-minute limit was placed on calls.

Fires or other emergencies could be announced, and help summoned, by an emergency ring of three sets of three, which sounded in all homes. Everyone picked up and the message was spread instantly so neighbors could assemble quickly to fight a fire. A more unusual service was the public notice. For one dollar, the operator would summon all subscribers to their phones with two long rings. If you didn't care to hear the announcement, you didn't answer that ring. But farms were far apart, days long, and few could resist hearing about the church social on Saturday night. Privacy was not as highly prized in a community where people depended heavily on one another, so it was considered a service when the telephone operator was able to tell callers that the doctor was at a particular house or that a neighbor was or was not at home. In 1940, on the death of her husband, Eunice Farr became one of the first women in the United States to operate a utility company.

With the opening of Mad River Glen ski area and later Sugarbush, the system was stretched to its limits. Long-distance calls, which were commonplace to the international patrons at the resort, had to be logged and billed by hand. New arrivals in the area complained of the lack of a dial system, and skiers from the city didn't like the party lines. At about this time there was a lot of pressure, too, from larger companies to buy out the Waitsfield system. The Farr family decided to stay put, and they switched to a dial system and single-party lines. But until 1964 the offices remained on the enclosed back porch of the Farrs' home.

The company continues to install the newest systems, now serving the increasing number of telecommuting residents, but local calls are still free on public phones. If you really need to make a coin call from Waitsfield, you'll find a phone that will take your money behind the Sugarbush Chamber of Commerce on Route 100.

Places to See, Eat, and Stay

The Inn at the Round Barn Farm, and Green Mountain Cultural Center, RR 1, Box 247, East Warren Rd., Waitsfield 05673; (802) 496-2276. Guest-friendly rooms, elegantly decorated, are located in the restored farmhouse and carriage sheds. Cross-country skiing available.

Lareau Farm Country Inn, Box 563, Route 100, Waitsfield 05673; (802) 496-4949 or (800) 833-0746. Rooms with private or shared baths in a rambling farmhouse with a comfortable, homey air. Sleigh rides in winter.

American Flatbread (located at the Lareau Farm, above); (802) 496-8856. All-natural pizzas baked in a wood-fired oven, served in an informal setting. Open year-round on Friday evening, 5:30 to 9:30 P.M.; July through mid-October also Saturday evening.

Palmer's Sugar House, Palmer Ln., Waitsfield 05673; (802) 496-3696. Open for maple sugar on snow and a look at a working sugar house, late February through mid-March. Syrup sold at the farm year-round.

Maple Spring Herb Farm, RR 1, Box 1770, Fayston 05660; (802) 496-3462. Open May through August; call for hours.

Sugarbush Resort, RR 1, Box 350, Warren 05674; (802) 583-2381. Sugarbush offers 110 trails for all skill levels on three mountains.

The Common Man Restaurant, German Flats Rd., Warren 05674; (802) 583-2800. Make reservations even in the slower seasons; there is nothing common about the menu offered by Chef Patrick Matecat.

The book *Snapshots: Waitsfield Vermont* offers a brief picture of the first two hundred years of Waitsfield history, with lively text by AnnMarie Simko, illustrated with vintage photos. Look for it among the selection of gifts offered in the lobby of the Inn at the Round Barn.

10
MONTGOMERY:
BOBBINS AND
BUTTERTUBS

(MONTGOMERY IS ON ROUTE 118, 32 MILES EAST
OF ST. ALBANS, REACHED VIA ROUTE 105 FROM
INTERSTATE 89 AT ST. ALBANS OR ON ROUTE 58
FROM INTERSTATE 91 AT ORLEANS.)

In 1776, when a military campaign was planned to invade Canada, northern Vermont was one vast wilderness, except for settlements along Lake Champlain and some newly opened grants along the Connecticut River. Between these two waterways, which would later form the borders of Vermont, lay thickly forested mountains and valleys. The success of the planned invasion lay in being able to get troops from the Connecticut River to the Canadian border as close to Montreal as possible.

General Jacob Bayley, who knew this territory better than most, determined to build a road capable of carrying troops and supplies through this forest from Newbury to Missisquoi Bay on Lake Champlain. Work on the road ended after the

Colonial victory that same year but resumed in 1779, when George Washington ordered it completed so troops could protect the northern frontiers from a British invasion through Canada—or, if necessary, to attack themselves.

Colonel Moses Hazen was assigned to the job this time. With a small contingent of men, he cut through the virgin forest and up and over the notch that now bears Hazen's name. Today, when traveling throughout the northeast part of the state, look for signs that point out a track that crosses the highway and runs out into the woods, identifying it as a segment of the Bayley-Hazen Military Road. The road was constructed of "corduroy," trees cut and laid parallel to form a bumpy but fairly solid surface. This road was little more than a cleared path through the woods, but even as it was being built it became the pathway of settlement. Route 58 from Lowell essentially follows the route of the original road.

The crest of Hazen's Notch is as far as the road went, at least officially, but over this rough track came, if not a steady stream of settlers, at least enough to establish a town with 34 residents by 1800. For a long time, this was the only route into the valley of the Trout River.

Today there are several approaches, all but this original one paved. But the dirt road through the narrow, almost pristine, notch and under its ledges is our favorite. From this wild landscape, which has changed very little since Hazen's forces hacked their way through it, the road drops into the village, passing brief stretches of cleared pasture and views of Jay Peak, to the north.

Today, approaching the town along this road you pass only a few farms high on the hillside above the southern side of the valley. During the last part of the 19th century and the early part of the 20th, this area was heavily farmed and was only one of several settlement areas in

Montgomery. The many farms here were prosperous and they were served by blacksmith shops, sawmills, and even their own school, at the corner where Amadon Road cut north across the valley.

While most of these farms are long gone, the hills are not deserted. On the south side of the road, about a mile from Route 118, is Zack's On The Rocks, certainly among the most eccentric dining places in the state. Zack, actually Jon Zachadnyk, presides over the dining room and the kitchen in a flowing gold-and-purple caftan and an abundance of gold chains. In the dining room the multilevel seating area has the appearance of a silk flower garden gone wild, while the lounge (where you are required to wait while your first course is prepared) is dominated by a life-size rag doll clad in an evening gown and a cardboard Bill Clinton playing the saxophone. The menu, if you can read the faded handwriting in the dimly lit bar, is varied and interesting, but not nearly as avant-garde as it was in the '60s, when Zack built here in a field of boulders. The experience is amusing, but expensive.

At the foot of the hill is Montgomery Center, where the Hazen Notch Road meets Route 118 and Trout Brook, turning abruptly into Main Street in front of the Community Baptist Church. Main Street, Route 118, stretches a bit over three miles from here to Montgomery. It may seem confusing to have two towns only three miles apart, both of which are named Montgomery (after the same Revolutionary general killed in Montreal). These two settlements are separate villages within the six-mile square political entity granted by New Hampshire Royal Governor Benning Wentworth. (Remember all the problems these early survey lines caused Dorset and the other western towns; at least here the mountains are around the edges, not in the center.) Montgomery, sometimes called "the village," is on the west, and Montgomery Center (sometimes called "the center") is on the east. Most businesses are in the center.

The Baptist Church at the head of Main Street was built in 1866, when the town was thriving and prosperous. Its Greek Revival style and white-columned facade, slightly elevated above the level of the road, give it a formal air, as though it were a schoolmarm looking out over a classroom. On both sides of Main Street are buildings that have served the town for over a century and a half as homes and businesses. At Christmas the church is decorated with a 20-foot wreath (pine boughs are in easy supply here) and lighted to become the focal point of the town's festivities.

Old photos taken from this spot show Rowley's Hotel just to the right, a bandstand, and an unpaved, narrow tree-shaded street, barely two buggies wide, with large houses set well back from the street. While idyllic, these photographs don't show the hard work and activity of the time, when a 10-hour workday in the veneer mill yielded 90 cents. Two of the photos reveal that Rowley's Hotel, with a two-story colonnaded porch on the front, was prosperous enough that a third floor was added within the few decades that separate the pictures. Now an apartment house, it is still one of the largest buildings in the community. Owned by an ailing former firechief, "Puffer" Lumbra, the hotel was renovated for him by townspeople as a token of their appreciation for his years of dedication to the town. Beside it, the Olde Livery hardware sits on the site of its livery stable.

The history of the building where you'll now find J.R.'s Restaurant and Pub is a good example of how businesses evolve in a small, isolated town. It started life as a school and then for many years served as a granary and hardware store. It has been an eating spot since the early '70s (including a stint as a nightspot called Natty Bumppo's). It is easily identifiable by the greenhouse dining area that jars somewhat with the surrounding buildings but does make a good place to have lunch and watch the activity on Main Street.

The three-story, mansard-roofed building almost across the street is Kilgore's General Store. This building has long been a center of commercial life here, having served such diverse functions as an appliance store and nightspot. The general store was opened in 1989 by people who wanted a store that actually served the needs of the town but still had the feeling of an informal gathering place provided by a soda fountain and wood heating stove. The second floor opens onto a balcony that looks down into the main floor below. The soda fountain is a real one. In the store you can get everything from plain breakfast cereal to gourmet foods, beer to French wines, souvenir T-shirts to plaid wool shirts. And although we personally wouldn't consider having breakfast anyplace but the Phineas Swann, we're told the breakfasts at Kilgore's are excellent.

Although Montgomery was originally a farming community, lumbering played a major role in the life of the town during most of the 19th century and the early part of the 20th. One of the most successful companies was the Nelson & Hall Company, owned by Charles Taylor Hall. Starting with a buttertub factory, Hall became a primary producer of the veneer used by the Victrola Company in the manufacture of hand-cranked phonograph players. Enormous numbers of oak, maple, and gray birch logs were boiled and then peeled by sharp knife blades on a lathe to make the large continuous sheets of veneer that were then taken by ox team to the railroad at East Berkshire.

C. T. Hall was so successful that he built himself an elegant mansion in town at the turn of the century. He also had a chauffeur to drive his Stanley Steamer, the first auto in town. His former home is now the Inn On Trout River, a few houses west along Main Street from Kilgore's. In addition to its 10 guest rooms, the inn has a well-respected dining room where you can have dinner by C. T.'s fireplace.

Next door is another of Hall's properties, this one built to house his household staff. The Phineas Swann is now a warm and comfortable B&B run by Michael Bindler and Glen Bartolomeo, the kind of innkeepers who obviously enjoy what they are doing. Although Phineas never lived here, he was an early farmer who lived in the hills to the north of town. The inn's four guest rooms are decorated with a lighthearted country elegance. Some share baths furnished with deep, claw-footed Victorian tubs, good for relaxing after a day of skiing. The wicker-furnished enclosed porch features a fascinating collection of autographed playbills and photos of theater greats. There is usually the big band sound of Glenn Miller or the Dorsey brothers in the background. A full breakfast often features fruit or preserves from the inn's garden beside the Trout River. Michael and Glen now have a restaurant license and will prepare elegant dinners for guests who make reservations with them in advance.

Even the owners of this successful small inn admit that living in Montgomery is a fiscal challenge. The area provides living proof of the not-so-funny bumper sticker: "MOONLIGHT IN VERMONT—OR STARVE." Nearly everyone does something else. They tap a few trees, keep a few cows, drive a school bus, make muffins for the store, do some carpentry, a little of this, a little of that . . . it all adds up. As Michael puts it, "People live here because they want to, not because their job is here. Making a living here takes creativity."

Marsha Phillips, for a time their neighbor across the street, is a good example of this kind of Vermont creativity. Several years ago she was searching for a business she could conduct out of her kitchen and came up with the idea of coating nuts with maple. From this grew the Mapled Nut Company. After several years of craft shows and convincing local stores to stock her candies, Marsha had stirred so many pots of nuts that she wore out her favorite wooden spoon. She decided to move out of her kitchen, although her only employee is still her mother. She took over a gift shop with a selection of country decorating and handmade items, moving her candy making to a kitchen in the back, and ran both businesses for a time. Now she and her pots of maple syrup are back in the family kitchen, but you can find her mapled almonds, walnuts, cashews, and pecans at Kilgore's and other places in the town where they are made.

Terry's Fine Woolens and Antiques is in a rustic barnboard-sided building a short distance away. Featuring Icelandic woolens, they also have alpaca ruana capes from Bolivia, and an interesting selection of antiques and related crafts. You will find the entrance to the shop toward the rear of the building on the left side.

If descriptions of tidy B&Bs, shops, and restaurants make Montgomery sound like a gentrified boutique town, we've misled you. Each one of these businesses has grown the hard way, with a lot of work by gritty people who were determined to survive in a town they liked. "If we'd wanted easy," one of them told us, "We'd be doing business in Stowe!"

Walking along Main Street today, you will find it hard to picture the town that was here between the 1870s and the 1930s. To the north and south you will see ranges of wooded rolling hills. At the beginning of the 20th century all of these hills were cleared, most used as pasture or croplands for the many farms that covered them. By the time of the Civil War, there were 160 farms with over 2,050 head of cattle. By 1880, the number of farms had risen to 187 and there were over 2,700 cattle on the farms in the valley and on the hillsides.

The product of all of these farms was milk, which in those days couldn't be shipped, so the milk was processed into cheese and butter to be sent to the cities and urban centers of the East Coast. The manufacture of buttertubs was born of this necessity and became a major industry in the valley from 1850 until the Depression in the 1930s. Large wooden mills were built in the center and in the village, along the banks of the Trout River, and the land along the banks was stacked high with the logs needed to keep the saws and lathes busy. Teams of oxen hauled sleds of logs to the mills and wagons of buckets to the trains for distribution to farmers in other towns around the state. And the oxen hauled the filled buttertubs from the hill farms to the trains in East Berkshire. Other mills located around the town used the logs for the production of bobbins of myriad descriptions to keep the woolen and cotton mills of New England operating.

Montgomery village also had a share of these tub mills along the banks of its streams. While most of the mill buildings are now gone, many of the houses there today were occupied by the workers who labored in them.

One of the early congregations in the town was the Episcopal Church, whose members met in private homes until 1835, when they dedicated their new Union Church, later called St. Bartholomew's, in the village. The congregation dwindled in the 20th century, and in the 1920s it stopped holding regular services. Its declining condition led, in 1974, to the formation of the Montgomery Historical Society, whose primary purpose was the restoration of the building. With an effort that typifies the community spirit of this town, the building was saved and is now the home of a museum housing a fine collection of artifacts, perhaps most notably a large collection of photographs of the town in its heyday. If you read the names on the old pictures and antiques, you'll probably recognize them as the same ones that are on the houses around the green today.

Close by, the Black Lantern Inn, with its unique double-gabled end facade, has been watching over the street since 1803. It is the longest serving inn in town, having borne several names and housed generations of "drummers"—businessmen and salesmen. The inn is still operating, offering lodging and dining to tourists rather than the rougher clientele of its past.

Montgomery village is also the home of another notable attraction, Montgomery Schoolhouse on South Richford Road, which has continued the town tradition of the manufacture of wooden items, in this case wooden toys. They pride themselves on the fact that these solidly built and brightly colored toys are virtually impossible to destroy. The factory sits on the site of the old village schoolhouse, and the steady growth of the company has helped firm up the town's economy.

Montgomery reached its greatest population in 1900, when 1,876 people lived within the town boundaries. Although the effects of the First World War led to a slow decline, there were still 1,386 people here in 1930. The Great Depression hit Montgomery, and as economic conditions plummeted, people left the farms. The tub factories finally succumbed to the pressures they had been under for the previous decade or so. Some of the mills burned, and with the fires went the jobs that had combined with farming to make a living possible. By 1970, the town reached a new low of 651 people, and in 1991 there remained only seven farms with 595 head of cattle. In 1994 only six farms were left.

But now there are skiers and summer visitors, bringing some activity to local businesses. Again, as happened two centuries before, it was the construction of a new road that made the difference. In the 1960s, the state built Route 242, which connected Montgomery to Troy and Newport and to Interstate 91 at the Canadian border. It ran past the ski area at Jay Peak, whose main clientele is Canadian. The road had two results. First, Canadian skiers could eat, stay, and shop in Montgomery, and second, skiers from farther south could now reach Jay Peak through the town.

Drawing from Montreal and adjacent areas of Canada, the ski industry sparked the development of second homes and resorts that brought tourism to the town for the first time. New stores opened directed at that market, and inns, B&Bs, and hotels blossomed. Montgomery's distance from the major eastern cities put it at a disadvantage for the ski market even though Jay Peak receives more natural snowfall (often more than three hundred inches a season) than any of the other northeast areas. Jay has a vertical rise of over twenty-one hundred feet and more than 50 trails.

Montgomery has another attraction no other town can boast, although they go largely unnoticed: a total of seven covered bridges, three of which stand above dramatic gorges. On South Richford Road the Fuller Covered Bridge crosses Black Falls Brook. Built in 1890 to replace a bridge that collapsed under the weight of a load of bobbins, it, along with the other six bridges remaining in town, was built by Sheldon and Savannah Jewett between 1863 and 1890. A local poet, Elizabeth Fuller, wrote of the age when they were built and their place in the community: "The bridge was once a haven on a rainy summer day. The children in the neighborhood would gather there to play."

The Comstock Bridge (1883) crosses the Trout River a short distance from the Black Lantern Inn, and two additional covered bridges, the Longley Bridge (1863) and the Hopkins Bridge (1875), are a short drive farther west on Route 118 toward Enosburg.

The natural beauty of the area and the recreational attractions are among the things that still do bring people who want a relaxed atmosphere among friendly people. One beautiful drive, or bicycle trip, is on West Hill. Take Route 118 south through the center less than three miles, then take Hutchins Mill Road to the right. After a short distance a waterfall appears to the south, just under Route 118, and a few hundred feet farther is the Hutchins Bridge (1883) sitting astride a falls and gorge.

Returning to Route 118, continue south to Gibou Road. Turn right, where you will cross the Hectorsville Bridge (1883). This one also sits astride a falls and at the head of a gorge. Continue on Gibou Road and take a right onto Hill West Road and follow it until you see an abandoned road leading steeply downhill to the left. Park and follow the road to the foot of the hill to the Creamery Bridge (1883), yet a third that sits over a falls. Be careful here, however, because there are serious washouts around the abutments of the bridge. By continuing on Hill West Road you will return to Route 118 northwest of Montgomery village.

While you are traveling these roads on West Hill, try to picture them as they were a century ago. Almost all of this land was open then; you could see down into Montgomery and pick out buildings. There were nearly one hundred farms, creameries, and mill buildings lining all of these roads. Now there is little more than a few scattered houses and heavy forests.

Montgomery Center offers another delight that only insiders know about: a swimming hole set at the foot of twin waterfalls, a cool and refreshing place to escape the heat of the summer. To get there, take Route 242 a short distance up the hill to the old (now abandoned) school. Walk between the school and the outbuilding and take the path that winds around down to the Trout River. But be careful not to litter or damage the environment, because it is private land that can, and will, be shut off if it is abused.

Places to See, Eat, and Stay

Phineas Swann Bed and Breakfast, Main Street, Box 43, Montgomery Center 05471; (802) 326-4306. Dinners by advance reservation.

The Inn on Trout River, Box 76, Main Street, Montgomery Center 05471; (802) 326-4391 or (800) 338-7049.

Black Lantern Inn, Montgomery Village 05470; (802) 326-4507.

Zack's On the Rocks, Route 58, Montgomery Center 05471; (802) 326-4500. Reservations required.

J.R.'s Restaurant and Pub, Main St., Montgomery Center 05471; (802) 326-4682. Serving breakfast 6:30 to 11 A.M. The chili is good, and the sandwiches generous. Inexpensive. Dinners served until 10 P.M.

Hazen's Notch Cross Country Ski Area, RR 1, Box 730, Route 58, Montgomery 05471; (802) 326-4708. The 30 kilometers of groomed trails and 120 kilometers of backcountry trails provide good conditions even when more southern areas have little snow.

Jay Peak Area Association, RR 2, Box 137, Jay 15859; (800) 882-7460 or (802) 988-2611.

11

PUTNEY:
TOLERANT AND
DOWN TO EARTH

(PUTNEY LIES ALONG THE CONNECTICUT RIVER,
JUST OFF INTERSTATE 91, EIGHT MILES NORTH
OF BRATTLEBORO.)

Putney's story has a lot more to do with people and ideas than with events and things. No military campaign began here, no Putney industry changed the world, no railroad baron chose to buy and restore it. Instead, Putney embodies Vermont's traditions of respect for differences and tolerance of new ideas. That's not to say that anything goes, but Putney has never been a town to look down its nose at the newcomer with a different lifestyle.

Its diversity is particularly surprising for a town with a population of only about two thousand people. This is a town where homes range from mansions to hard-put trailers. It's a town of large and small farms, craftspeople and mid-size industry.

Putney's character and its tolerance shine through the story of John Humphrey Noyes. Noyes was born to well-to-

do parents in Brattleboro in 1811 and moved to Putney with his family in 1822. While in college, he encountered a little-known religion called Perfectionism, and in 1834 he declared himself to be a Perfectionist. This faith held that Christ had already appeared for the second time, and that after conversion people were free of all sin. Noyes became such an exponent of the faith that he is sometimes considered its founder, since his tenets displaced the earlier ones. In time these beliefs developed into a combined religious and social philosophy, and he formed his Perfectionist Community in 1838. He, his wife, and several other relatives pooled their inheritances of $38,000 and set up what he called a "Bible Family" in which all were equal, all property was held in common, and all contributed to the mutual welfare.

By 1843 Noyes's experiment in communal living had attracted 28 adults and nine children who lived in the group's houses, worked their two farms, and worshiped in their own chapel on Main Street. Their number grew to almost 150 by 1847. George Bernard Shaw said of the Noyes Perfectionists that they were "one of those chance attempts at Superman which occur from time to time, in spite of the interference of man's blundering institutions."

Members of the group got along well enough with each other and with townspeople, but we get the first glimpse of the reason for their ultimate departure from Putney in a letter Noyes published in 1837. In it he said, "In a holy community there is no more reason why sexual intercourse should be restrained by law, than why eating and drinking should be—and there is as little occasion for shame in one case as in the other." This meant that the sect practiced what Noyes called "complex marriage," in which each man was married to all women in the community and each woman was married to all of the men. Noyes and a few select leaders decided who was allowed to mate, and those not selected were expected to remain celibate.

Apparently Noyes's words of 1837 didn't reach Putney for a decade, for it wasn't until 1847 that people in Putney became aware of what was going on in their midst. Indignant, and probably also inspired by the revivalist spirit that was sweeping New England at the time, the citizens of Putney filed complaints of adultery, and Noyes was arrested in October 1847. He slipped away to Oneida, New York, before his trial, and was joined there by a large number of his followers. In Oneida the community was reestablished, and it launched several commercial businesses, including the manufacture of silver plate. "Complex marriage" continued to complicate the lives of community members, however, until they abandoned it in 1879 and Noyes withdrew to Canada.

While the sexual practices of the Perfectionists may have shocked the people of town when they finally figured out what was going on, the Communist philosophy of the Noyes group didn't seem to bother them at all. Sharing of property, while a strange notion, was okay, but sharing wives went a little too far. Even to rock-ribbed conservatives of the mid-Victorian era, the then-strange Communist philosophy of their neighbors was their neighbors' business. Violation of the family was another matter.

Putney and the towns immediately south of it along the Connecticut River are unique in having been part of five states, or, more accurately, four colonies that later became states and one independent republic. In 1716 Massachusetts and Connecticut settled their common border. Massachusetts ceded to Connecticut several thousand acres, and Connecticut granted to Massachusetts almost forty-four thousand acres of "equivalent" land on the west side of the Connecticut River. This land that moved from Connecticut to Massachusetts now encompasses Putney, Dummerston, Brattleboro, and Vernon. Later, Massachusetts and New Hampshire settled their borders and jurisdiction over the "equivalent lands" passed to New Hampshire. Then New York claimed it, until the Revolution, after which it was part of the independent Vermont.

As early as 1733 people from Connecticut came up the river to harvest the mast pine that grew thick and tall along its shores, particularly at a spot known as the Great Meadow. Here the river made a long broad turn around a flat terrace that rose above the water. While a fort was built on the Great Meadow in the 1740s, the settlement did not last and was abandoned at about the time of the siege of Charlestown, New Hampshire, across the river, in 1745. In 1748, New Hampshire Royal Governor Benning Wentworth made a grant of three townships created from the "equivalent lands," and another fort was built in 1755 on the Great Meadow. Settlement still lagged because of ongoing attacks during the French and Indian Wars. Finally in 1762 a town was laid out by the proprietors, and by 1765 fifteen families were living in the town.

New York then made claim to "the wilderness," or the New Hampshire Grants, and in 1766 declared these grants void and gave the towns three months to apply for a "confirmatory" charter. In plain language, that meant they had to pay off the State of New York. While many other towns resisted the New York claims, particularly on the western side of the grants, Putney was one of three towns that did buy its New York charter.

Even after they'd paid, however, New York sheriffs were still summarily tossing settlers out. In 1775, settler Andrew Graham reported that ". . . a Number of Persons headed by a Deputy Sheriff under New York without ever producing any writ came and Draged your petitioner with his family . . . and turned them into the Naked Wilderness and put one

Benj. Wilson into possession of your petitioners house . . . and that Said Benj. Wilson . . . did in the course of the winter now Last past leave his wife and family and run off with a prostitute to enjoy her in that Government which has So long Countenanced his wickedness here . . ."

While Andrew Graham had no use for the Yorkers, the majority of the people in Putney sided with New York. They were not only at odds with the defenders of the New Hampshire Grants, but with the Green Mountain Boys as well. In 1775 they even raised a New York militia and the strong feelings between the New York adherents and the New Hampshire grantees led to a bloody confrontation at the courthouse in neighboring Westminster. Ethan Allen weighed into the fray with his Boys and prevented the meeting of the New York Court there.

With the peace that followed the end of the Indian wars, the centers of settlement moved away from the river to places along Sackett's Brook in Putney Village and Minott's Brook in East Putney. The end of the Revolution accelerated growth. While the river has been the roadway for the products of the early settlers, highways soon began to appear over the hillsides, and settlement moved up into the hills. The brooks were soon recognized as sources of power and put to work.

The first gristmill operated on Minott's Brook in 1765, followed by another on Sackett's Brook the next year and several more in the years to follow. One of these mills, on Sackett's Brook, was founded by the father-and-son team of Orrin and Charles Thwing in the early 1800s and operated until 1946, grinding as much as fifteen thousand bushels of grain a year. Close by, a number of sawmills also took advantage of the cheap and plentiful power of the rushing water.

While large-scale manufacturing was never part of Putney's economy, the great period of sheep raising in Vermont led to a textile mill to turn the raw wool of the neighboring farms into woolen fabric. The Putney Woolen Company was a part of the community from the early 1840s until 1876, when it closed its doors. The sheep raising and wool processing continues today, however. On what is probably Vermont's largest sheep farm, up to 2,600 animals graze on land that was once was part of the Great Meadow.

Oak Grove, a shop on Main Street, has a wide variety of yarns from their own farm and other farms in New England. Wool varieties such as angora and merino, kid mohair, llama and alpaca are all available, and are almost all hand-dyed. Raw fleece can be custom-milled and dyed to the customer's specifications. Green Mountain Spinnery, on Depot Road on the south end of town, is another source of yarns, particularly wool and mohair, which they produce in the smallest spinnery in the United States. In addition to yarns, the shop sells patterns, and scarves, hats, mittens, and blankets that are hand-knit and woven by local craftsmen.

The small paper plant in the center of Putney sits on the same site where paper has been produced since 1818. The largest employer in town, the Putney Paper Co., has been twice destroyed by fire, in 1938 and 1946, but has continued to provide a core of employment. The company has kept up with the times and has a large, newer, plant on Depot Road for processing recycled papers.

Since its beginning, Putney has been a center of small business and industry, enterprises usually with one, five, or a dozen employees engaged in marble production, blacksmithing, tanning, carriage building, clock making, and the myriad of other crafts that made products needed in local homes and farms. And, to keep all that industry fueled, they also had as many as seven distilleries operating at one time. A couple of ingenious locals boys devised a horse-drawn rake that was among the first attempts to mechanize farming, but it never resulted in a local industry.

In 1842 Cassius Wilson started a business that has continued to prosper and is now "the world's major producer of genuine American splint baskets." Basketville, on the north side of Sackett's Brook along Route 5, occupies a large new store with every conceivable type of basket from all parts of the world. They still produce their own in the factory across the street, where they offer tours showing the process, which begins with the logs of ash trees. This small-town factory has eight stores in six states all the way down the Atlantic coast to Florida.

In the 1960s, more than a century after Noyes and his commune lived here, Putney's tolerance and willingness to let others live their own way was still alive and well. As the war in Vietnam wore on, the war protest movement led many to reject the norms of mainstream society. The counterculture that sprang from this group sought fulfillment in home-steading, subsistence farming, and crafts. Some chose to follow these goals as individuals, others as part of groups with varying degrees of communalism. Putney, possibly because of its past relationship with an alternative philosophy, attracted a number of people who shared this outlook during the 1960s and '70s. They have remained in the community and enriched it, all in harmony with neighbors who may or may not agree with their political ideas. The results are still evident in the roster of cottage industries, many of which have become widely recognized businesses. Randi Ziter, manager of the Putney Inn, proudly claims that Putney has the highest concentration of artists and craftspeople in the northeast.

In addition to the fabric crafts represented by the two wool spinneries, the hills of Putney are scattered with studios. The Putney Woodshed sells the work of over 130 artisans, many of whom are from the Putney area. Their varied stock includes unusual boxes and kaleidoscopes, drums, instruments, wooden toys, miniatures, garden statues, and books on Vermont. Two craftsmen specialize in furniture making. Zellmer's Cabinets, just up the street from the center of town, has been custom designing and building cabinets and hand-carved furniture for more than 25 years; Richard Bissell makes fine Shaker-inspired pieces, Windsor chairs, and cabinetry at his workshop on Signal Pine Road.

On Kimball Hill, just a short way from the general store, Doris Fredericks runs a workshop and showroom where she makes and sells stoneware and pottery. Her shop, the Putney Clayschool, has pitchers, bowls, trays, plates, pots, animals, and just about everything that you could make out of clay. A few doors up from the general store, Offerings sells unique handcrafted jewelry and individually designed gifts made from silver, semiprecious stones, and other media. Sigrid Scherm Pratt custom designs and installs Kachelhofen, tile stoves usually associated with northern Germany and Scandinavia. They are noted for their exceptional efficiency.

Each year the craftspeople and artisans of the area hold the Putney Holiday Craft Tour and Sale on the weekend after Thanksgiving. The tour takes you into their studios and includes works in clay, glass, wood, fiber, and iron.

Putney's community spirit was here long before the influx of the 1960s. The Putney Cooperative Food Store, on the south end of Main Street in front of a retirement home, is a good example. Founded in 1941, when the prospect of food shortages loomed large, it is among the oldest food co-ops in the state. Even before you get into the store you know that this is more than a store: it's a community meeting place. Along the covered entry walk is a long bulletin board that serves as a local newspaper. If you want a well-used Volvo, private dance lessons, classes on the theory of herbal medicine, a cat, a baby-sitter, or any one of hundreds of other services or products, this is where you'll find it. The co-op sells many local products, including organically grown vegetables, as well as a full line of groceries and other items usually found only on the shelves of a city deli. The co-op also has a deli counter where you can custom design your sandwich on fresh, home-baked breads, either to take out or eat in their informal lunchroom/café.

While the culture of the sixties lives on, so does the even older world of the small-farm owner, mechanic, and mill worker. Right in the center of the village, where the road up Kimball Hill leaves Route 5, and across from the paper mill, the Putney General Store is not only a classic village store, but a sort of modern department store at the same time. Look at the rough and unfinished floors, and you will see where the walls used to be, as this store has expanded since opening in 1843. The slow undulations of the floor aren't looked upon as an inconvenience so much as a fact of life. The store caters to the varied needs of the village, carrying not only the basics and convenience food, but a respectable supply of ingredients for Mexican, Thai, and other cuisines—and one of the most complete spice and herb shelves around. On the second floor are video rentals and a health department that would rival that of a major chain. The lunch counter features a marble terrazzo counter and fountain, serving sandwiches and specials such as baked chicken, mashed potatoes with gravy, corn, and a beverage—for five dollars.

For all the variety of lifestyles evident along Putney's main street, it still retains its village air. The Putney Federated Church is a beautiful example of the classic New England church, with its sanctuary on the second floor and common rooms on the lower level. Original 16-over-16 wavy paned windows still look out under the two-tier steeple.

Putney was the lifelong home of George D. Aiken, a man who for decades seemed to symbolize Vermont and its heritage of intelligent, independent politics. George Aiken was born in 1890 and lived his youth on a farm on Putney West Hill. A farmer, he began the cultivation of berries and fruit-bearing plants. When they began to reproduce, he couldn't bear to throw them away, so he sold the surplus plants from his farm.

Along the way he became fascinated with wildflowers, ultimately publishing *Pioneering with Wildflowers* in 1933. He dedicated the book, which is now a classic on the subject, to Peter Rabbit in hopes that "the little rascal will let our plants alone from this time on." He was a nationally recognized expert on the subject and was among the first to sell wildflower seeds and promote their landscape uses. His successes as a plant propagator ultimately required that he open Putney Nursery, on Main Street near the food co-op.

George Aiken's life would have been considered a full one if he had rested on his laurels as a writer and plantsman. But he became a state legislator, lieutenant governor, governor, and, in 1941, a U.S. senator. In the Senate he was noted not only for his independence, but also for his expertise in agriculture. He was an early champion of the creation of the St. Lawrence Seaway, the massive joint U.S.-Canadian project that turned the St. Lawrence River and the Great Lakes into international ports.

The senator, usually and lovingly referred to as "Governor" by Vermonters, was a frequent guest in the dining room at the Putney Inn, a country inn in an old farmhouse on Depot Road. He was such a fixture that, even after his retirement in 1974, the inn staff didn't find it unusual when he went about the dining room greeting diners and talking with them about Vermont. A room has been dedicated to him and displays some of his memorabilia, including the plaque that was presented to him at the time of his retirement from the

Senate. The dining room, presided over by award-winning chef Ann Cooper, is a popular place to eat, drawing its clientele from a wide radius.

While all of southeastern Vermont has a long and outstanding connection with the performing arts, Putney has its own very special offerings. Each summer during July and early August, the Yellow Barn Music Festival brings outstanding chamber music concerts on Tuesday, Friday, and Saturday nights. Pianist Janet Wells and her cellist husband, David, cofounded the festival, which showcases internationally acclaimed and young rising artists.

During the 1960s a brand-new campus was built for Windham College, but economic hard times came and Windham couldn't keep up the payments, so the college closed. When the campus later became Landmark College, which specializes in the education of people with dyslexia and other learning disabilities, a group of area residents with a deep interest in theater took over the college's theater and made it into the River Valley Performing Arts Center. They host a wide variety of events throughout the year.

In addition to Landmark College, Putney is home to other noted educational institutions. In 1937 the Experiment in International Living moved its headquarters to Putney. Its purpose is to foster international understanding and respect, and it was among the earliest of the exchange programs to send Americans to live with families abroad and to arrange for foreign citizens to live and travel in the United States. The Putney School was founded in 1935 as an independent secondary school. It emphasizes not only a stimulating curriculum, but hard work and play, the arts, and study abroad as a means of creating "the whole person."

In a way, that pretty well sums up the town's philosophy, too.

Places to See, Eat, and Stay

The Putney Inn, Depot Rd. (at Exit 4 of Interstate 91), Putney 05346; (802) 387-5517. Lodging and fine dining are offered in the old inn with adjacent motel facilities.

Hickory Ridge House, RFD 3, Box 1410, Putney 05346; (802) 387-5709. A B&B in an elegant 1808 Federal farmhouse off Westminster West Road.

Patch Road Cheese Company, David & Cindy Major, RFD 3, Box 265, Putney 05346; (802) 387-4473. Sheep milk cheese, semi-hard aged, a five-pepper blend, and a mellow rosemary.

Basketville, Main St., Route 5, Putney 05346; (802) 387-4351.

Green Mountain Spinnery, Box 568A, Putney 05346; (802) 387-4528. Off Depot Road at Exit 4 of Interstate 91.

Richard Bissell Fine Woodworking, Signal Pine Rd., Putney 05346; (802) 387-4416. The studio is located off Westminster West Road.

Zelmer's Cabinets, Kimball Hill Rd., Putney 05346; (802) 387-5948.

Holiday Craft Tour & Sale. Call (802) 387-4481 late November, 2 to 5 P.M.

12

WOODSTOCK: TOO GOOD TO BE REAL?

(WOODSTOCK IS 14 MILES WEST OF
WHITE RIVER JUNCTION ON U.S. ROUTE 4;
SOUTH WOODSTOCK IS FIVE MILES SOUTH OF
WOODSTOCK ON ROUTE 106.)

The complaint is often made by Vermonters that Woodstock is not a "real" Vermont town. Their point is that money, and plenty of it, has infused the town with an air not just of prosperity, but of city people playing at being country gentry. Rather than being a Vermont theme park, as many say of the tidied-up village of Grafton, Woodstock, they claim, is just not Vermont at all.

The same charges have been made, in one way or another, against other towns in the state—Manchester and Arlington come to mind—which only proves that although these towns may not be like every other town, they are a part of the state just as real as the Green Mountain Boys and skiing.

If those who would scrub Woodstock from the roster looked closely at the town's past, they might understand that

this legacy of wealthy benefactors is part of its history, too—
a legacy that has been shaping the face of the village for very
close to two centuries. For many of Woodstock's patrons are
seventh generationers.

Only 20 years after the first settlers arrived in 1765, Woodstock became a shire town, the seat of Windsor County. As
such, its position was assured as a center of government and
its related commerce. From the first, people had to come here
to do business with the court or county officers, to record
and investigate land titles, to probate wills.

Because it was already the center of so much activity, it
was natural that other enterprises should spring up here, and
its green and main street were soon lined with businesses offering silverware, hats, tailoring, breads, and other goods and
services. Twenty of these surrounded the green itself, and
more shops filled the streets that radiated outward from it.

Mills and manufacturing grew along the streams and
rivers outside the center of the village: grist, saw, cider,
fulling, woolen, oil, and carding mills opened, along with an
iron furnace, tannery, distillery, brick kiln, and dye house.
Even flutes and pianos were made here, and no fewer than
five weekly newspapers flourished. But no one industry pre-
dominated, either physically or economically.

To this center were attracted not just the lawyers who did
business with the court, but other professionals and merchants, who built fine homes like those they had left
behind in the cities of Connecticut and Massachusetts. By 1800, Woodstock was already a so-
phisticated cultural center. Because this
prosperity continued, as did Woodstock's reputation as a good place to live, those homes
were kept up and cared for, and many of them
can still be seen along the town's streets.

One of the lawyers who settled in town at
the end of the 18th century was Charles

Marsh, who served in Congress and as attorney general under George Washington. His son, George Perkins Marsh, also a lawyer and a congressman, became one of the first conservationists with the publication of his book *Man and Nature.*

Meanwhile, Frederick Billings moved to town with his father, who sought a fresh start here after a financial reversal. The penniless young Billings probably never dreamed that he would someday own the fine Marsh home, but after hanging out his shingle as a lawyer on San Francisco's infamous Barbary Coast during the Gold Rush, he made a fortune in his practice and in real estate. When he returned to Woodstock, he bought the Marsh estate and raised Jersey cattle on his farmland, importing the first of that breed to be brought to the United States. He was interested in land management and conservation, and he planted trees to replace those lost to earlier timbering. He kept up his business skills as president of the Northern Pacific Railroad, and he endowed schools and churches.

Frederick Billings's granddaughter, Mary French, married Laurence Rockefeller, and together they have continued the work of the Marshes and Billings to preserve the land around Woodstock. Their interests include the building and operation of the new Woodstock Inn and Resort. They and their company, Rock Resorts, have been active in preserving local properties, often purchasing or subsidizing and restoring them as housing for resort employees. It was Rockefeller who paid to have the telephone wires in the village buried to maintain its early appearance.

The farm where Frederick Billings raised his Jersey cattle is still a working farm, open to visitors as Billings Farm and Museum. Along with the barns, sheds, and shops of an active farm are exhibit areas and the home of the farm's manager. In the creamery downstairs is all the equipment used to make butter and cheese. Throughout the year the farm holds special events, many of which highlight seasonal activities on the farm.

Other benefactors have made it possible for historic properties and collections to be displayed so the public can glimpse at Woodstock's rich past. In 1944 the very active historical society purchased the Federal-style brick and frame house on Elm Street that had been built by a prosperous merchant in 1807. It is now a museum of local history, with collections of furniture, art, historic toys, costumes, textiles, and such everyday items as kitchen utensils and farm equipment in addition to the restored rooms of the Dana home.

Is there a price for all this largesse? Locals are mixed in their views, but those who live outside the village proper point out the difference in government between the village, which is run by its own trustees, and the town as a whole, which is managed by the selectmen. Many town residents feel that the village people "want to pretend they'd still be a pristine little place without the tourists," which, they add, is utter nonsense. They cite the delight village police take in ticketing out-of-state cars "for traveling one mile an hour over the speed limit. No warning, just a fine." Tourists, they say, are angry and won't come back, which hurts the whole town, whose livelihood depends on tourists.

Lest all the public-spiritedness leads you to believe that every native son of Woodstock was a benevolent philanthropist, we should balance the record with some notorious rogues. As Lee Dana Goodman puts it in her lively book *Vermont Saints and Sinners*, "In Woodstock, counterfeiting seems to have been a cottage industry." At the turn of the 19th century, when America's own currency was new and people didn't have much confidence in it, foreign money, especially Spanish, was used extensively. In Windsor County, it was also created extensively, and court records show convictions of at least nine counterfeiters, some of whom operated as a ring.

Visitors seeking a less rarefied Woodstock should drive south on Route 106, along the Kedron Brook, to South Woodstock. Or better yet, approach it first, as we prefer, from the south, allowing it to unfold in a series of well-kept farms leading into a village of historic homes clustered around the brick stagecoach tavern, which rises directly ahead at a sharp bend in the road. Especially at night, when the Kedron Valley Inn is lighted, it's as impressive an entrance to a town as you'll find anywhere.

Although this "South Parish," as it was called when it was settled only four years after its parent town, is nicely cared for and prosperous, it has more of the feeling of a village and less of being a nicely landscaped shopping mall than Woodstock. There are no boutiques in South Woodstock; in fact there is only one store, the busy market alongside the inn.

There used to be more stores, and one of them, built by a man named Ransom, now serves as an annex to the inn, which has individually decorated rooms that make the most of the quirky interior architecture. One room is on two floors, the upper of which was opened up from a closet, where the stairway leading to it had been cleverly disguised. The room had been used by Ransom, an active abolitionist, to conceal runaway slaves on their route to Canada.

The main building of the inn, a busy stagecoach stop owned by James Slayton, also active in the movement, was another Underground Railroad station, with a hidden cellar underneath what is now the dining room. Current owners Merrily and Max Comins found it when they were renovating. "If you climb onto the shelves in the cellar, and through a hole in the stone foundation, there's a crawl space cut out, then a five-foot drop into a hole," Max says.

A large ballroom once extended over carriage sheds between the two buildings, used for local meetings and social events. The dance floor was built on rubber balls to give spring to the steps of the dancers. Cotillions were held there, grand affairs that were the highlights of village social life. The museum at the Academy displays dance cards from these.

Fiery abolitionist meetings took place there as well. One of these was interrupted by a group not so in tune with their fellow Vermonters' antislavery sentiments, and the assembly summarily pitched the intruders out the second-story windows and continued their meeting.

South Woodstock continues to retain its identity as a separate village, although its residents take part in town events, hold town offices, and are otherwise active partners with the larger village. In the days before it was only a few minutes' drive between the two, the social life of South Woodstock was more distinct, with a variety of local societies meeting at the inn and in the homes of members.

In 1815 a group of young men founded a "Literary Fraternity" in the South Parish, with more than 30 members dedicated to improving their minds and developing their judgment in social values. To this end they debated current issues, including the rights and roles of women in society. They were quite liberal for their time, voting after the debates that women should own property in their own name and be educated equally with men. They subscribed to a broad range of current publications, which the members shared. Before that, a library had been formed, by subscription of its members, to provide books in the village.

The Kedron Brook, which formed the valley in which the village lies, was lined with small mills, including a sawmill and tannery owned by Frank Standish. Upstream, along the coach road where Route 106 now runs, homes, farms, and workshops used the brook as a convenient disposal system, pitching in whatever they didn't want and waiting for the high water to carry it away. In the spring of 1871, Standish placed the following advertisement in the local paper: "Our neighbor Standish would esteem it a favor if all the residents along the South Branch would throw all their refuse, garbage, brush, etc. into the stream, as the quantity that now comes down to the flume is not sufficient to keep one man employed constantly to keep it clean."

A walk through the center of South Woodstock is not only pleasant, it is a trip through the architecture of the 19th century. A few of the buildings are from the 1790s. The large building on the hill was built in 1848 as the Green Mountain Liberal Institute. It was begun by a group of Universalist ministers and laymen for the education of their children, who came from all over New England and beyond. Its purpose was to educate young people without the religious bias prevalent in the traditional education of the time. It later trained teachers. In the summer, the Academy Historical Association operates a small museum in the building.

Travelers interested in antique textiles and quilts should plan to stay at the Kedron Valley Inn, where they can see the outstanding collections decorating public areas and guest rooms. The 60-plus antique quilts, a collection that began with the innkeeper's own family quilts, are museum quality, and constitute one of the largest collections in the state. Each quilt is labeled with information about its history, often with anecdotes of family history as well. In addition to the quilts, fine examples of vintage needlework are exhibited in frames or are in use throughout the inn. Most guest rooms have original hooked rugs designed by Claire Murray, and all rooms have quilts.

Several pieces of the collection are displayed in the dining room, but don't expect to notice them after your appetizer is served. The cuisine of Chef Jim Allen will command your full attention there. The inn has built a reputation for fine dining; here, as elsewhere, we look for the evening's specials. We think these show chefs at their most creative, and they often use ingredients that are not available year-round.

Although many of the houses in the village of South Woodstock date from the 1700s, they could be nearly new compared to the possible origins of a structure on nearby Morgan Hill. Throughout New England, usually located on hilltops, are more than two hundred stone chambers, each with one of four astronomical alignments, and of a nearly identical construction. Several of these lie along what is called "the Celtic High Road," which runs through South Woodstock. The largest and best preserved of them is on Morgan Hill, within sight of the road. Although it is on private land, it is accessible to those with an interest in prehistoric sites (and to those who scoff at the whole notion).

The structure is solidly built of stone, covered with a mound of earth. Its roof slabs weigh several tons each. A square hole in the far end is directly over a small stone platform. The sighting from this spot, through the door, points exactly to the place where the sun rises through a low notch in the eastern hills on the morning of the winter solstice. Each of the other similar structures points to the winter or summer solstice or one of the two equinox sunrises.

Most academic historians and archaeologists scoff at the suggestion that these structures are of prehistoric origin and usually dismiss them as root cellars built by local farmers. But this theory doesn't explain the similar inscriptions in them, the hilltop locations, the astronomical orientations, or the massive ceiling slabs. Nor does it explain why only certain farmers built root cellars in this particular and nearly identical way, while all the others built them whatever way fitted the terrain or their own particular needs. The academics' explanation also fails to explain the abundance of standing stones, basin stones, and other unusual formations nearly always found close by. Nor does it account for why these particular cellars should so closely resemble the sites of known Celtic origin found throughout Europe.

We'll probably never know for sure if these were built by Celtic mariners three thousand years ago or by ambitious farmers who hauled three-ton stones for sport, but after exploring this structure and reading about the others, we found it hard to dismiss the possibility of a prehistoric explanation. To get to the site, turn east off Route 106 at the fire station and drive to the top of the hill. Look for a gate on the left, just over the crest of the hill; park at the gate and follow the farm road. The structure is on your left and you can see it from the road. And do remember this is private property.

Even those who, like us, opt to enjoy the quiet hospitality of South Woodstock eventually gravitate at least once to the action in Woodstock. The town offers plenty to do and see, with plentiful tourist services. They ought to: they've been welcoming visitors since their early days as a shire town. But tourism as an industry was late coming to Woodstock—in

The Windsor County Court House, On the Green, Woodstock

fact to Vermont as a whole. The first tourists who took vacations in New England and New York came to the springs, and it was hard for businesslike Vermonters to understand why someone would come if they weren't sick. A vacation was an alien notion to people who had to milk cows every day.

So when the people of Woodstock decided to take advantage of their beautiful setting and try to attract travelers, they thought they'd need a mineral spring to entice them. Someone remembered that in the 1830s there had been a spring on the side of Mount Tom, which overlooks the village, and that its waters had been used to cure kidney trouble and dyspepsia. So Sanderson's Springs was "rediscovered," cleaned out, and enshrined in a springhouse. It was christened Sanatoga Springs, in a not very subtle attempt to capitalize on a very successful older competitor in New York.

A 15-acre park was built to surround the spring, with rustic bridges, bridal paths, a hilltop gazebo, wooden stairways, and walking paths. Only then did investors feel secure in building the resort hotel. The Woodstock Inn would have succeeded without the spring, but it was just too much for a Vermonter to believe. The spring is now long forgotten, but the inn, several buildings later, still thrives as a full-service resort.

Forty-four years later another hillside event in Woodstock was to change the economic—and physical—face of Vermont. Winter sports had long been popular in the area. A winter carnival with competitive events, sleigh rides, skating parties, tobogganing, and gala winter parties had made the Woodstock Inn a year-round resort since its opening in the 1890s. Skiing was beginning to catch on, but only with a limited number of real enthusiasts, mostly members of the newly popular college outing clubs. For these hardy youths, climbing up the mountain on skis was part of the sport. But it clearly wasn't for everyone.

Then, in 1934, a group of skiers rigged a rope tow powered by an old Model T engine on a hillside at Clinton Gilbert's farm in Woodstock. Purists scoffed that the sport was ruined, but the idea caught on. It was the first rope tow in America, and it marked the beginning of the ski industry. It also put Vermont firmly on the map as a year-round vacation state.

The winter carnivals are no more, but the annual Wassail celebration the second weekend in December is a community event that visitors are welcome to join. With the trees and windows lighted and shops decorated for the holidays, the town becomes a stage set for the parade, the weekend's highlight. Down the main street and around the green parades a steady line of horse-drawn carriages and wagons, including a goodwill wagon, which is filled by townspeople and visitors with gifts of clothing and food for families in need.

Christmas brings to mind another of Woodstock's unique features, its five Paul Revere bells. Two are displayed where they can be seen by passersby—the oldest on the porch of the Congregational Church, and another at the Woodstock Inn. The others are in the Universalist Church, the Masonic Temple, and St. James Episcopal Church. No other town in America has as many as five Revere bells.

Places to See, Eat, and Stay

Kedron Valley Inn, South Woodstock 05071; (802) 457-1473. The inn's 27 guest rooms are located in three buildings on 15 acres with a beach on a private swimming pond.

Woodstock Inn and Resort, On the Green, Woodstock 05091; (802) 457-1100. With pool, downhill and cross-country skiing, golf, tennis, and a full indoor sports facility, the inn combines a resort with a village setting.

The Billings Farm and Museum, Route 12 and River Rd., Woodstock 05091; (802) 457-2355. Open May 1 through October 31, daily 9 A.M. to 5 P.M. Call for weekend schedule in November and December. A museum shop sells books about Vermont and farming, as well as period gifts and craft kits.

Dana House Museum and Museum Shop, 26 Elm St., Woodstock 05091; (802) 457-1822. Open mid-May through late October, Monday through Saturday 10 A.M. to 5 P.M., Sunday 2 to 5 P.M. It is also open on a limited schedule in the winter, but you should call for times.

Academy Historical Association, South Woodstock 05071; no telephone. Open July and August, Saturday 3 to 5 P.M.

Kedron Valley Stables, P.O. Box 368, South Woodstock 05071; (802) 457-1480. Escorted trail rides; inn-to-inn riding vacations; surrey, wagon, and sleigh rides. Just up the road from Kedron Valley Inn.

The Wassail parade is held the second weekend in December, the highlight of a weekend of activities. For parade information, call the Green Mountain Horse Association at (802) 457-1509.

Vermont Saints and Sinners, by Lee Dana Goldman, is published by New England Press in Shelburne, Vermont, and is available at bookstores throughout the state for $9.95. It is filled with the exploits of Vermonters and includes overviews of both the mineral springs and the role of Vermont in the Underground Railroad.

INDEX

ABOUT THE AUTHORS

Stillman and Barbara Rogers are New England natives who have hiked, skied, bicycled, and driven in all corners of Vermont since childhood. They are the authors of *Natural Wonders of Vermont*, *New Hampshire Off the Beaten Path*, *The Rhode Island Guide*, and three books on the Atlantic Provinces of Canada, in addition to two books on Europe. They are contributors to *Yankee Magazine*'s *Guide to New England* and write travel pieces for several magazines and newspapers. When not traveling, they live on a small farm in the Connecticut Valley and raise herbs, which they sell at the Brattleboro Farmers Market.